Pat[i]

I w___ ___ ___ ry
about 25 years ago,
I haven't read it

my
mother's
tattoo

in over 10 years.
I'm thinking about
reading it at our
family Seder.
    I hope you
enjoy reading it.
Happy Pesach
& lots of love
Norman
(& Andi)

3/29/19

my mother's tattoo

&

other family memoirs

Harry Applewhite
Debra Bohunicky
Karen Gegax Campbell
Laura Bowers Foreman
Norman Glassman
Glenn A. Leichman
Claudia Lewis
Carol Lanie Riley

Pod Publishing - Mercer Island, Washington

Pod Publishing
P.O. Box 1124
Mercer Island, WA 98040-1124

Quatrain 158 by Rumi, translated by John Moyne and Coleman
Barks, is reprinted by permission of Threshold Books, RD 4 Box
600, Putney, Vermont 05346.

Printed and bound in the United States of America

Library of Congress Catalog Card Number: 95-72982

ISBN: 0-9649568-4-5

pod *n.* A group of mammals in community; a school, as of dolphins or whales. The community of those authors whose essays appear in *My Mother's Tattoo and Other Family Memoirs.*

We dedicate this book to families and writers everywhere.

Contents

Acknowledgements

This book could not have been put together without much patiently-given computer advice from Gordy Gegax.

John Engerman graciously undertook to give vision and form to our cover needs.

We especially thank Audrey Lewis for getting a tattoo, and for generously permitting us to use a photo of her with her twin sister.

Becca Robinson thoughtfully read and commented on early drafts of our manuscripts.

Our deep gratitude goes to Brenda Peterson, who taught us that writing is an act of community.

Foreword

Brenda Peterson

Memoir is a most intimate relationship. First there is the complicated dance between writer and memory, a partnership in which the writer makes an invitation to the past, convinced he or she will certainly lead—and ends always following memory's strong, sure and surprising steps. We surrender to remembering stories that often make real sense of our lives and of those people who, if preserved with compassion and care, become major characters right alongside us. For even though the memoirist usually writes first-person, the world remembered is full of characters who rival the writer's own reality. In this way there can be a generosity to writing memoir—as the narrative eye/I serves more as a guide, allowing the reader to feel and see with us, and to sometimes *become* us.

Over the years that I've worked with the students who contributed their family memoirs to this anthology, I'm sure they wearied of my reminding them that the opposite of self-consciousness is generosity, that the antidote to dismemberment is remembering, and that the epiphanies we make of our own lives can offer others the hard-earned wisdom that we all seek to share through stories. I often imagine that authentic, honest storytelling, even if it takes us to the darkest fathoms of our being, is naturally illuminating—like those bottom-of-the-ocean creatures who give off their own light as a by-product of simply exploring such depths.

I have watched these writers plumb their own pasts with courage and curiosity as well as the companionship of their classmates. It is one thing to enter alone these sometimes treacherous shoals and sudden drop-offs; it is another to dive into the deep sea of one's own true stories with the support and insight of fellow and sister writers. In gathering this anthology, each writer engaged in many hours of dialogue with this community of writers—sometimes as cheerleaders, sometimes as concerned critics. I imagined that in the first drafts the writer was a scuba diver descending alone while we above held firm the anchor and the breathing lifeline. After the story was gleaned like so much sunken treasure, we helped to shine and decipher just exactly what it was that the writer had discovered. And often the final story displayed here went through many sea-changes in which the entire community decided to dive down with the writer and play and explore together, true to naming themselves after a pod of whales or dolphins.

We chose family memoirs because they are our first stories and often our most vivid, before we forget or deny or forgive without even knowing what it is we are letting go. And here is another way in which memoir is a most intimate bond: Our characters, drawn from our lives, are sometimes not content to simply be created by us. They can talk back; they pick up the phone upon reading their lives filtered through our writer's imagination and they argue with us, disown us, call us to account, and sometimes congratulate or thank us. Unlike the fiction writer, the memoirist must truly face his or her characters if they are still alive and this adds another dimension to both the writing and the publishing of family memoir. There is a poignance to this double partnership—between writer and memory and between writer and other's memories of the same shared territory. Sometimes we have spent class time in a dialogue about the writer's responsibilities to real people and events, about the effect of our stories on those who embody them. A guideline in this community of writers has always been that, to use Dante's words, "All evil comes from perverted love," or George Eliot's description of the bond between tragedy and misunderstanding. The writers in this anthology are not victims or even heroes, they are refreshingly open about their own shadows and there is almost always the attempt to understand the heart of even the most disturbing character. There is also the instinct to celebrate the small moments when characters connect and confide. Upon reading one of these stories in which she found herself profiled, a mother actually drew closer to the writer and claimed that she felt finally understood and fully met on the page.

Each of the stories in this anthology reflect poignant images of mothers and fathers and brings to light the profound, many-layered experience of parent-child relationships. The title story of *My Mother's Tattoo* is Claudia Lewis's celebration of her mother's life—it is the grown child's tribute to the success of an older woman's reclaiming of her life, her independence and happiness. Harry Applewhite's "Mother Touch" is a son's reckoning with an ailing and vulnerable mother. This son's story explores the healing power of touch and subtly acknowledges the reciprocity of the life cycle. Laura Foreman's memoir vividly recalls her father's near-death, and her simultaneous loss of innocence. Glenn Leichman's "My Father's Secret" describes his startling discovery of a haunting episode in his father's past; and the author's sadness for his father and fear for his own young son. Carol Lanie Riley's story is the only one written from the perspective of the parent, a single mother who lost a son and is determined to remain close to the other even as he embraces a religion that excludes her beliefs. Norman Glassman's memoir also faces loss, but in the context of an important Jewish tradition. Amidst the ritual of his family's celebration of Passover, the author reflects on his comprehension of his father's cancer and his long-time denial of his imminent death. Karen Campbell's story, "On Finding," is an honest portrayal of her difficulty in accepting her mother's schizophrenia. The last memoir, "Zen Mother" by Debra Bohunicky, is a devoted testament to a spiritual mother figure and the author's valuable lesson of humility.

In all these family memoirs there is the theme of reconciliation and a search for understanding the Other, through story. Perhaps for any writer there can be no more healing, illuminating, and exhilarating an act than making sense of the swirl of memories that surround us. So here is an invitation to join in this intimate dance of memory and community and story-making.

—Brenda Peterson
Seattle, 1995

My Mother's Tattoo

Claudia Lewis

My mother and her identical twin were born in 1919. There's a quick, syncopated rhythm to that date, a good year for duos. The twins slept in matching cribs parked alongside each other in the upstairs front bedroom. My mother remembers afternoon naps in that crib, when she would wake up to look for her sister, who was waking up, looking for her. My mother swears she and her sister never fought. Their communication with each other was telepathic and as unselfconscious as the right arm swinging with the left. Though their primary identification was as twins, each had her own personality. My mother jokes that she became a big-city mouse, while her sister became a country mouse, baking perfect pies for her big family.

Today my mother is seventy-six years old. She's vigorous, good-hearted and unpredictable. Her eyes are blue; her hair is silver. She's short, barely five feet tall, and getting shorter. Her broad behind has gone flat, "the better to sit with," she says, thinking of a comfy chair and a stack of good books.

Now emotionally widowed—my resourceful father having lost his way in the terra in-firma of Alzheimer's disease—my mother is living alone for the first time in her life. She had been married for more than fifty years, and before that she had had her life with her twin. So it is only now that my mother is able to appreciate the pleasure of her own company.

What surprises me is how unorthodox that pleasure is.

"You won't believe what I just did," my mother announced one afternoon not too long ago. I love getting phone calls from her that start like this.

"I've always wanted to get a tattoo," she continued—but this was news to me. I sat up, alert.

She had found Blue Moon Tattoos in a part of town where her quilter-friends and bridge group would never go. She parked her snazzy convertible close to a Harley hog, but not too close. She dropped her keys into her pocketbook and snapped it shut, and then, taking a breath for courage, walked nonchalantly into the waiting room. She browsed through pictures of serpents and flames and skulls she could choose to be hers forever. She sat down. A hairy-chested man in a black leather vest with a grizzly bear snarling on his muscled bicep was sitting across from her. The man's look was not friendly. For an instant my mother felt out of place and wanted to leave.

"Did it hurt much?" she ventured.

"Oh, lady, it hurt like hell!" he complained, grateful for her interest. She smiled; he relaxed, and they talked tattoos.

My mother got tattooed. She says it wasn't painful, only irritating. Later, because I remained cool to body art, she reminded me that her perspective on forever is different than mine. A colorful butterfly rests its wings on her left shoulder. She says she did it just for fun, but I like to think it's proof a free spirit still animates her age-spotted body. My mother shows it only to her most liberal friends because she is not interested in criticism.

She got enough of that from her mother. My grandmother was not only overly critical but also self-centered and sometimes brutal. Even as an old woman, Grandmother could still fix her hard, mean eyes on us in the way she had as if to brand the word *stupid* on our foreheads. For my mother, as a little girl, that look meant a frightening trip down into the basement, back where it was dark and cool, back where the canned goods and jars of pickles were stored, where dust burned on the single lightbulb that swung from the end of a short, black cord. There my grandmother would stuff rags in my mother's mouth so Mrs. Althons, who lived next door, couldn't hear. And then she would beat my mother with her wooden-soled slipper.

Sometimes it was my mother, sometimes her twin, who was jerked down those stairs to the basement when no one else was around. One or the other might be safe for awhile, but only until some mishap put them in jeopardy of their mother's fierce anger.

It was my mother's greatest joy to be an identical twin, a joy Grandmother could never diminish. And when my mother speaks of her three older brothers, she closes her eyes and smiles, experiencing again sweet memories of mutual devotion.

"We would do anything for our brothers," she tells me, referring to her childhood self in the plural. "We used to play this game, when Mother was out. My brothers would get us to jump off the stairs—and they were steep!—that went up to the second story. Mary was just a little timid and wouldn't go much higher than the middle. But I would. Those boys would get me to jump from the next highest and the next and I'd do it, jumping right into their arms," and as she tells me this I can feel her little girl heart pounding, her little girl body awash with her own daring.

"Then I'd be at the very top of the stairs, looking a *loooong* way down, and my darling brothers would be cheering me on: 'You can do it! You can do it!' And by God I would do it. And they did catch me, every time, just like they promised."

The brothers grew up, going on to universities, pursuing their careers. And the twins, too, were able to go away together for a few years of college. The sisters also fell in love together, a coincidence of heart that they were able to celebrate in a double-wedding ceremony.

I love to look at the photographs of this dazzling affair. My mother and her sister stand in the extravagant swirl of their white satin gowns. Both smile identically beautiful smiles. In other pictures I see their young and confident husbands and their handsome brothers, everyone so proud. Even Grandmother looks pleased.

The photographer focused on the brides. But his film could record only the spectrum of light seen—and not that of Destiny, sunken-eyed and patient, lurking in the background. No one knew then that my mother's sister and brothers were being stalked by depression, marked for early death.

Mother was forty-five years old when her sister committed suicide. My aunt had moved in with us after her husband had died from a brain tumor. She brought her two youngest children with her. Devastated by the sudden and unexpected death of her vigorous husband, she had tried to kill herself even before she came to us.

Decades later I can still recall that bright, sunny, California morning I went down to breakfast. I had just turned eighteen. My father was already at work. My sister was away at college. My mother was brewing coffee as her sister slept upstairs. This was the first time in a very long time that my aunt had been to our house. So despite the tragedy of her brother-in-law's death, my mother was pleased to have Mary's company.

Sweet rolls were baking in the oven, the pecans just beginning to turn brown under a glaze of cinnamon sugar and butter. My mother squeezed fresh oranges. And waited for her sister to come downstairs. She adjusted the napkins and silverware and poured out three glasses of juice, saying, "Why don't you go up and see what's keeping Mary?"

We had plans to take Mary's two little boys to the zoo that morning. They had finished breakfast early and were playing outside.

I felt my mother's enthusiasm as I took the stairs, two at a time, up to Mary's room. The door was closed. I knocked lightly, softly calling her name, "Mary?"

Not only was the door closed but there was no light coming out from under it.

"Aunt Mary?"

I recall the hallway where I stood and the dormer windows that faced west. I turned the knob quietly and opened the door. I could just make out Mary's small form beneath the covers, but she was too still, much too still. Wary, uncomprehending, I stepped closer, my eyes compensating for the inadequate light. I bent forward to peer into my aunt's face, which was also my mother's face, now strangely gray. And then I heard myself wail, "Oh, Mom! Something's wrong!"

My mother ran up the stairs and rushed past me to her twin, to kneel by the bed, listening for life.

"Mary," she pleaded.

She alone heard the faint rattle of Mary's last breath, her unwilled good-bye. She had taken a fatal overdose of sleeping pills.

My mother called an ambulance. She had me shepherd Mary's little boys to the neighbor next-door where they wouldn't see their mother's body being taken away. My mother followed the ambulance to the funeral home. I found myself in our empty kitchen, mindlessly prying the sweet rolls off their brittle glaze.

For my mother, losing Mary was like having her right arm ripped off. Isolated in her grief, she missed the one person she needed most. I was only a bystander to her pain, watching helplessly as my mother carried the burden of her dead twin.

Today the tally of those who have committed suicide has risen to five; subsequent generations stay current with the language of emotional disorder as we track the depression that veins through our troubled family. While I have never felt suicidal myself, I hate driving across high bridges, afraid that some overwhelming urge to die might sweep me over the edge.

For the last thirty years I have often wondered how my mother and her twin, who were so alike genetically, could be so different in temperament. My mother wakes up every morning, glad to be alive, determined to live her life fully. Especially now that she has fallen in love again.

She met a man her age who finds her attractive, who laughs at her jokes, and who doesn't always win at gin rummy. They met through the Garden Society and are considering a trip to Hawaii together, to see the orchids. "I've got my own life to lead," she says. And she means it.

My mother willed herself to outlive her own mother, and she did, the only one of five children to do so. But more importantly, she has out-loved her mother, loving her family, her friends, loving the good parts of her long marriage, and now loving herself.

Last February she came to Seattle to see my family and me, one by one showing us her tattoo. Oh, geez, I thought to myself, now my kids will want one. Purple hair can grow out but a tattoo is forever. Peering sullenly from under their cloud of immaturity, my three teenagers wondered who invited this grandma to join their exclusive rebellion against convention. They were puzzled by her late urge to bloom. I hoped it was her *brio* that impressed them, that and her jolt of originality.

Then she stunned me by wanting to drive all the way back home to Denver, across the Rockies, across four states, alone, in the middle of winter. I ranted against this terrible idea. There was a break in the weather and the fools at my motor club conspired against me by suggesting that she could go now, or wait until spring.

"But she's eighty years old!" I exaggerated.

"She'll probably make it if she leaves today."

I was not reassured. Nevertheless, she wanted to go home. I fixed up an emergency kit of sandwiches and candy bars, filled the windshield-washer reservoir with fluid and stuffed my down jacket between the seats. She had already faced her demons, this woman who is now comfortable in her own company. Ignoring my visions of blizzards and catastrophe, she backed her convertible down our driveway, waved good-bye, and declared, "Honey, I'm tail-light!"

Even though a clogged fuel line stalled her in Oregon, she did make it home, terrifically pleased with herself. She knows her sister would have been proud. Now my mother is busy entertaining, reciprocating the parties she attends. She has lots of friends but I can't say they appreciate her. It's hard to guess what they thought when she stuck a glass ruby to her forehead and went to a sophisticated dinner party. Shrugging her shoulders, my rebel mother explains, "I don't know why I did it; I just felt like it."

Not a worrier, she's always ready for adventure. Recently we were in Mexico together and I can recall standing on the beach, holding her just-signed risk disclaimer, while she tossed back a shot of tequila and then was strapped into a harness attached to a power boat. The tow line tightened and she hung on, catching her breath, the wind in her fine gray hair, as she parasailed up and away, hooraying back to me, "I did it!"

I admit I haven't always appreciated my mother. There was a time when I was a boy-crazy rock-and-roller that I thought I actually hated her. In those days I rejected even the possibility of a resemblance between us. But now at fifty, I find myself becoming more and more like her; my hands look like her hands, and sometimes I sound just like her. I hear it when I answer the phone or when I laugh, which is more than okay by me.

We call and write and visit each other often. But there are difficult times in her life. She copes on her own, not affiliated with any church or pastor. "Religion," she says, "raises more questions than it answers." She does hope that when she dies her sister will be waiting for her at the end of a long, dark tunnel that she sees in her dreams. Sometimes I wonder if she catches a glimpse of Mary in the gold framed mirror that hangs above the console table in her entryway.

Because I'm deeply grateful for this secure and loving place where my mother and I now stand, and because I'm not so sure that anyone waits at the end of any tunnel, I don't like it when I catch my mother looking beyond me. I notice it when she says, "I want you to have this ring now, so I can enjoy your pleasure in having it," or, "Do you think the kids would like my luggage?" I feel her turning away from me when she dismantles the photograph albums, sending each of us favorite snapshots. I want to cry out, "Don't go there!" as if I could hold her back. "Mom, do you hear me? Don't go there," I plead with her in my mind, cradling this twin who taught me love and tethered me to this world, this woman—my mother—who defied her family destiny, this maverick spirit who chooses to be happy.

Mother

Touch

Harry Applewhite

"Oh, my throat's so dry," she said, after I kissed her gently on the cheek. Her bright blue eyes matched her robe. Only a few gray strands blended with her brown hair. Mom was in Saint Vincent Hospital in Santa Fe, hooked up to oxygen. Though she's ninety, and had been hospitalized for several days, she didn't appear tired or weak. I wanted it to be a good visit, so I resolved to avoid our deep racial and political differences. Conflict wouldn't be good for her heart. But when I'm around Mother, the racial subtext is always there.

"Last night I thought my back was broken," she said. "This morning when the doctor came, I told him about my back. But he wasn't too concerned."

"Does it still hurt?" I asked.

"Just a little," she said.

I wanted to do something to help, to give her a massage, which I knew she would like, but I held back. I felt uncomfortable. I had never massaged her before.

"Could you get me some water?" she asked, her voice strained by dryness. As I reached for the nearest glass she snapped, "No, not that glass. It's dirty."

Her tone and the words carried me back to the kitchen of our home in New Orleans. I was eight, and about to pour a drink of water, when Mother had said, "Not that glass!" She waved her finger, scolding me like an angry schoolteacher. "That's Alice's glass." Alice was our maid. "You might get syphilis!"

I didn't see how I could catch syphilis from Alice's washed clean glass, and not from the gumbo she fixed for our supper. I realized for the first time that Mom's fear wasn't because Alice was our maid, but because she was black.

I poured Mother's water. She had been on her way to Seattle to see me, my adult children, and her new great-granddaughter. She had stopped to sightsee and visit relatives in Santa Fe, but the 7,000-foot altitude had disturbed her heart. Her doctor advised her to return home. Mom needed my help, and I was glad I was free to give it.

We left for North Carolina early on New Year's morning. Arrangements had been made for oxygen during the various stages of the trip. As our plane flew over the Blue Ridge mountains, Mom said, "They are so beautiful. How could you leave them?" For twenty years Mother has focused on this question, not on my answer.

"These are beautiful," I said, "but I like the big, rugged mountains of the West and I love the water of Puget Sound." Sensing her disappointment at my answer I continued, "But the Blue Ridge mountains will always be part of my life, thanks to you. It's a gift I'll cherish forever."

I closed my eyes and drifted off to another memory of the South. In the mid-1960's I drove with four others from Illinois to Montgomery to march with Dr. Martin Luther King, Jr. The march, the music, the speeches, the hot sun, the humidity, the trooper who stopped our car and harassed us, feeling safe eating and drinking with blacks, not whites. It all came flooding back. The white-haired couple in their seventies from Rock Spring, Virginia, the black mother with the broad smile and the missing front tooth who marched, even though she would lose her job if the family for whom she cooked and cleaned found out. I remember the waving hands, the cheers from people standing along the street. I felt free, part of something bigger than myself. A river of justice carried me.

Racism was everywhere, in the workplace, the schools, the restaurants, the churches. I didn't want racism to keep hurting the black people I knew. Racism was in my family. My mother and father, though not hecklers, were ashamed that I was in the march. Even though my mother and father had been kind to Alice, especially if she was sick or in trouble, they would have fired her if she had marched.

Racism was in me, too. I didn't want it, but I didn't know how much its presence had shaped me. When I first saw a white woman and a black man holding hands, I felt a jolt in my heart. It was a painful discovery. In the middle of the march I started to ask, was I walking to free others, or myself?

On the march we all joined hands and sang,
Deep in my heart, I do believe,
We shall overcome someday.
And it happened. The song came alive and something stirred in me. I became part of something more powerful than racism. I knew somehow, some way, justice and love would overcome. But I didn't know how arduous the struggle would be, or how long it would take.

As our plane began to descend, I wondered how much my passion for social justice had been a response to the God I worship, whose name is Justice, and how much was a rebellion against a mother who couldn't let go. "That's grace!" I thought. "Justice uses us, cluttered motives and all, for larger purposes." I glanced over at Mother, wishing that she had marched with me, or that I had been bold enough to invite her.

Hours later, in the full care retirement community where Mom and Dad had retired, I sat in the chair in which Dad had spent so many hours after his stroke and before he died. From the window I could see the entrance to the apartment complex. I knew why Dad had liked to sit there. "People who can't move need to see people who can," my mom said. This chair was a good place to do that.

I looked around the living room. It was not a large room, perhaps fifteen by ten feet. There must have been nearly a hundred objects, hung on the walls, displayed in hutches, or on tables. Even though the room was crowded, it didn't feel cluttered. There was a story behind each object.

"Where did you get this painting, Mom?" I asked.

"My Great-aunt Mary gave it to me," Mom said. Her face broke into a broad grin and she suddenly looked ten years younger.

"I remember Aunt Mary's eightieth birthday party, held at a fancy Louisville restaurant. Aunt Mary climbed up on top of the table and danced a jig! Then, still standing on the table, she pulled out a cigarette and lit it up. It made quite an impression on me."

"Did she have too much to drink?" I asked.

"Well, I don't think so. She was just like that. Always doing something unusual."

I wondered if there was a touch of Aunt Mary in Mom that had been buried all these years. Did the strictures of Southern culture hem in my mother more than she realized? If she had married a man from New York, not Mississippi, would she have danced on dining room tables?

We looked at a photo of an old plantation home, a romantic symbol of the Southern culture Mother had embraced. "You should have stayed in the South!" she complained.

Nothing has changed. For over thirty years she's said this to me every time I visit. Mother has never forgiven me for not returning to the South after graduating from Yale Divinity School. But if I had received a call to a church in the South, it wouldn't have been easy for Mother. I would have wakened her to the social revolutions she slept through. "Look where God's leading the New South," I would have said. Even now I can feel her embarrassment when her friends discovered my God was different from theirs.

The night before I left she woke me at about 12:30 A.M. "Can you put some icepack cream on my back?" she asked.

"It hurts. I think my vertebrae are cracking."

"Sure," I said. She had mentioned back pain to the doctor in Santa Fe, but he hadn't been concerned about it, so I wasn't either.

As she handed me the cream, I said with amazement, "Mother, your fingers are longer than mine. Especially the little one."

She didn't believe me, but when we measured, her little finger was almost an inch longer. Surprising, since I'm six foot one-and-a-half, and Mother, in her prime, was barely five foot two.

"When I was a child, people told me I had the hands of a musician," she said. Mother had taken piano lessons, but it takes more than large hands to become a good musician.

There was an awkward silence as I hesitated. Boundary fears stirred in my stomach and tightened my throat. I had never touched Mother's back. Was it okay this time?

I was about to ask, when she groaned in piercing agony, "Oh, it hurts so much to be old." Her raspy groan rattled in my heart, driving out all but her pain. The lines on her face sagged until she seemed one hundred and fifty years old. I had never seen her so vulnerable, never felt so much of her pain. I knew my hands needed to be healing hands. There were no other hands to help.

She handed me the cream and lowered the back of her robe. "You've never seen a back so wrinkled," she moaned.

"It's not wrinkled," I said, vanilla wafting to my nostrils as I rubbed her back. "It's smooth and soft." It felt like the skin of someone much younger.

"My neck hurts," she said, pointing to her neck, throat,

and the top of her chest. I found the wrinkles on her neck. The skin was tougher, with tiny ridges, not soft and smooth like her back.

The lines in her face softened and her eyes became less anxious. I remembered my body had been inside her body. Her womb had been my first home. She had nurtured me for nine months. When she gave birth to me, she fed me with sweet milk. Now, as my hands nursed her, soothing her hot pain with cream, I felt something deeper than myself flow slowly, gently, through my hands, my fingertips, then to her. The healing touch reached beyond her back and neck to warm both our hearts, as our struggles faded away. The rough waters of our spirits ran still, and the surface peace went deep. She was my mother, and I was her son.

The Lessons of Lilies

Laura Bowers Foreman

Family came to the old Bowers house for an afternoon of iced tea and stayed six months. I was five years old as I watched the kaleidoscope of kinfolk breeze by. Sweaty, belted, round relatives puffed through the kitchen, always with a caramel or coconut cake tucked under a freckled, flabby arm.

I loved to go to my grandparents' old house in Canon, Georgia. There I could shed my skin as an only child. Dipping into this world of cacophonous children was so unlike my calm childhood. While the adults drifted around the house and porch, catching up and comparing, I romped with my spirited cousins.

Canon looked like a ghost town, but it was full of life. Prior to the Depression, the train delivered cars filled with salesmen working the cotton-circuit between Atlanta and Savannah. But by 1961, the town had been returning to the soil, brick by brick. The old house was the exception; it seemed to rock along with each generation.

This visit was to be my family's last for quite awhile. My father, Hurst, had been promoted and was to be transferred to France. I was to enter the world of first grade in this distant land. My days of sweet childhood were coming to an end.

My father, built like a bulldog, impatiently charged through his life. His compact muscular body flickered with constant alertness. Accustomed to the urgent schedule of a pilot, he was unable to relax, even on vacation. The eldest of four children, Dad considered his aging parents to be his personal responsibility. Seizing each moment as an opportunity to achieve and accomplish, he spent the six-week-long visit building and installing kitchen cabinets. The suffocating, sticky heat of late summer swirled with the thick kitchen stove steam and Dad's ever-present cigarette smoke.

It was a summer morning like every other during that vacation, but before Dad could enlist me once again as his project's go-fer, I scooted outside. My cousins were playing hide-and-seek in the intricate and tangled yard. Joining them, I scrambled to hide. Quickly, I ducked behind my grandmother's regal lilies and climbed through the dark, ancient forsythia.

Panting quietly, heart pounding, I listened as each of my cousins was discovered. Feeling an itch, I glanced down to scratch my mosquito-bitten ankle. A skull stared back at me, and its canines seemed to lunge for my sandal. Paralyzed in place, I screamed at this specter of death.

Fearing the worst, a deadly snake bite, adults and children came running from every corner. My father arrived first and scooped up his terror-stricken daughter. Just as he was about to ask what happened, he saw the skull. Without words, he carried me to the cool comfort of the screened porch. He sat down with me on his lap. The cool blue of my grandmother's trellised morning glories washed over me. I buried my head against his chest pocket, inhaling hot cotton and Kent menthols.

Rocking me gently, my short summer-scratched legs swaying with his rhythm, my father explained, "That was an old dog. He fell into the goldfish pond a long time ago and couldn't get out. My daddy buried him over behind the playhouse. I guess it just wasn't deep enough. I'll go out and take care of it." He spoke quietly, trying to calm me.

Occasional sobs shuddered through me, upsetting my silent swaying. My aunts set the lunch table. They seemed to be swirling around me with platters of tomatoes, bowls of mayonnaise and baskets of cornbread. I scrunched up my nose, inhaling the strong aroma of stewed turnip greens. "Where's Mommy?" I whispered.

"She's upstairs getting a bath. She'll be down after while." Dad sat me down on the wooden chair beside him. Everyone piled into the little screened porch. My family ate lunch with their usual uproar. Patting my shoulder gently, Dad quietly got up from the table. The screen door slammed as he went out to rebury the dead. I remained quietly locked in my terror, unable to erase the image of the dog's skull.

Later, Dad asked, "Honey, why don't you come and lie down?"

Foregoing my usual defiant, "I'm not tired!" I obediently went into the cool room and climbed up onto the white knobby bedspread. I fingered the smooth, worn cotton between the soft bumps. I thought silent prayers with each bump, like rosary beads on a string. "Please take care of that dog, God. Why did he die? Please keep him in heaven with you. . . ." But despite my prayers, the dog's grin of horror haunted me.

Pillows propped against the iron headboard, Dad tried to read a magazine. I sought the comfort of his strong arm. He winced with pain. Rubbing his left arm, he grimaced as he explained to me, "Honey, don't touch that arm, it really hurts." Readjusting myself, I watched as the cigarette smoke swirled around my father's head. It seemed to be lifting him heavenward. I drifted off into a deep sleep.

As I slept, Dad gingerly shifted positions, trying to relieve his pain without waking me. He put his hand to his chest, his breathing was shallow. Quietly, he rose, leaving me to my rest. He struggled out onto the porch. His father greeted him, "Well, Hurst, come on out and sit with me for awhile." He motioned for my dad to pull up a rocking chair.

Holding onto the back of the chair for support, Dad turned to his father and said, "Daddy, I have to go to the hospital."

My father, mother and grandfather all raced to Royston,

the next town, about five miles away. The small, rural hospital was one story, low to the ground. The red brick radiated long, lazy heat waves, making the building quiver with menacing life. Mom hurried inside and with few words, frantically grabbed a nurse and wheel chair. Dad was quickly wheeled into the emergency room. The swinging doors flapped shut leaving my mother and her father-in-law with the useless task of waiting.

The house was silent when I awoke. Never had I heard such quiet here before, never. I called out, "Daddy? Mommy?"

Cousin Berthine slipped in with a smile. "Well, you've been asleep for a long time. I bet you feel better. Everybody had to leave, but I stayed here to be with you."

Still sleepy, but feeling cleansed from my earlier terror, I asked with innocent curiosity, "Where did they all go?"

Berthine, Dad's cousin via a complex web of family relations, was about twenty years his senior. She led me outside, her tall, sturdy frame bent with the burden of her knowledge. She shepherded me toward the comfort of the porch. The echo of Berthine's blue eyes and high cheek bones sang quietly on my face. Swinging gently on the long porch swing, Berthine brushed a wisp of gray hair from her forehead and began to explain about her young cousin, only thirty-seven years old, and his heart attack.

"Honey . . . your daddy got real sick while you were sleeping. He had to go to the hospital. Your mama's there with him. We're just gonna have to wait to find out how he's doing. But I'll be here with you, darlin'." The crape-myrtle beside the porch railing cast an eerie pink shadow as I listened, and I felt my innocence spill onto the wooden floor.

During the next two days, I watched family members huddle together, cautiously whispering. They took turns going to the hospital. My grandmother wandered around the house, her noble elegance soaked with fear and sorrow. Those first few days, my mother did not leave her post by Dad's bedside.

The family finally decided I must see my father, just in case the unthinkable happened. Visitors under twelve were not allowed at the small hospital. A nurse, realizing our plight, brought a wooden crate outside Dad's hospital window. The crate tipped precariously as I stretched on my tiptoes trying to peer inside. The rough brick windowsill scraped my arms as I tried to stabilize myself. Berthine wrapped her long, embracing arms around me, offering security and strength. My face pressed against the screen while my eyes slowly adjusted to the dark room.

I saw my father sleeping quietly under white bedding. His strong, familiar arms rested beside him, one held prisoner by a seemingly endless array of tubes. I muttered the words I had heard explained to me over the past two days, "Heart attack, heart attack." My five years of life could only provide a cartoon image of a crazed Valentine attacking my daddy.

This was the first time I had seen my mother since this nightmare began. Fear arced from my mother's face to my heart. I had never seen her afraid before. Tears streamed from her gentle brown eyes, down through newly formed creases. Her smile seemed frozen in place. She stood up and held her brown hand against the screen. I pressed my small hand against my mother's through the indifferent metal mesh. My frightened eyes were veiled behind the window screen. Wiping her cheek, my mother turned to my dad. He lay there silently, his life masked behind closed eyes.

Gently, she touched Dad's arm. "Hurst, can you see who's at the window?"

Slowly, he opened his eyes, turned his head and smiled at me. The bed was quite close to the window, but it seemed miles away. I listened as his words wrapped around me like an embrace. "Hi, honey. Sorry they won't let you come in. I'll be okay soon."

Like a June-beetle, I clung to the brick, afraid to look away. I ached to reunite with the love and security I had played in only two days ago. Strange antiseptic smells mingled with the sweet scent of my grandmother's lilies beside the bed.

I felt hands wrapping around my waist. A seemingly distant voice spoke, "Come on, darlin', we better go now. Your daddy needs to rest." Lifting my limp body, Berthine removed me from the window. She carried me gently to the car.

The next week passed with numbing occupation. My cousins finally turned off the T.V. and returned to their play, the work of children. I sat listlessly by the ample magnolia tree. I scooped up handfuls of powdery soil and began to build a grave-like mound. Quietly, I gathered blossoms from my grandmother's garden and sprinkled the blooms like holy water. I watched as the lush petals of the lilies curled into a mournful amber pile.

Each day my mother returned from the hospital for short

visits. She cradled me and I clung to her, gulping up her love. Words seemed hollow as we rocked together. My mother closed her eyes and hummed softly as she stroked my smooth, straight hair. I rhythmically ran my small finger over the ridges of her strong fingernails. These brief reunions filled me with a brew of hope and fear.

Berthine tried to fill the void of my parents' absence. "Come on outside, sugar, I want to show you something." I obediently followed her through the cool, dark rooms as we made made our way outdoors. I had convinced myself that following in cautious obedience would lead me out of this dream-turned-nightmare. If I could do everything just right, I would be allowed to wake up.

The screen door creaked open and slammed shut, as it always did, singing the refrain of the old house. I squinted in the bright daylight. The heat and late summer fragrances swarmed around me. I passed my grandmother's lilies, great voluptuous bouquets that were like a party of beautiful women everyone whispered about and feared. My stomach tightened as their fragrance teased me with memories of the hospital room.

The garden, once a haven, now seemed menacing. The lilies parted to reveal the cruel goldfish pond. I stiffened as I imagined a ghost-dog struggling, hopelessly entangled in the stems and leaves. This was no longer a safe sanctuary.

My cousin continued to guide the way. Kneeling down and caressing my small shoulders, Berthine pointed up to a little wooden bird house hanging from a low branch in the pear tree. The ripening pears adorned the tree like ornaments. The ground was littered with nibbled fruit. "Do you see that little house?"

I nodded.

"Climb up on this box, honey, and take a look inside. I want you to see the nest of baby wrens. These babies are full of new life. Death will always be around us, child, but babies, they always bring us hope."

Still squeamish, I timidly began to ascend. I tried to secure myself on the shaky crate, and not disturb the bird house. Berthine supported me with her steady strength. I cautiously leaned on her.

The opening into the bird house was a small, dark hole. I peeked in, tilting my head, trying to see inside the little shelter. Then I heard their whispers. As the sunlight filtered in, I leaned forward to glimpse the bobbing, bald babies, hungry for life.

Many years have passed since that frightening summer. My father survived, but my mother and I became the guardians of his health, always alert for that shadow of death that had come so close to all of us. My solitary childhood taught me a cat-like self-reliance, but I have realized that my own life could be brief, should my health mirror my father's. I have learned to live with my family's dark clouds of ill health. Constantly struggling against death's threat, I search to find love, find life.

My

Father's

Secret

Glenn A. Leichman

My father was a self-made man, a Russian immigrant who rose up from poverty to become a successful child psychologist. He had a thriving practice, and in the 1960's he became a regular guest expert on "Art Linkletter's Houseparty." He would interview small children, dazzling the audience with his uncanny ability to coax children into talking with him. The parents of these children must have thought my father had a special gift, for he was allowed access to secret parts of the children's psyches.

One day when I was twelve, I accompanied my father to the studio and sat in the audience, watching him record the show. It was exciting to go to a real television studio. I also got to spend some time with my father. We drove to the studio in silence, the sun streaming in through the windows of the family sedan. I couldn't think of anything to talk about on that warm summer afternoon. But then, I never could. I wished that my father would have been as interested in my life as he was in the lives of the children he interviewed. We drove on, lost in our thoughts. I stared wistfully at my reflection in the window and watched my childhood pass by.

As soon as we arrived, I went up and sat down at the back of the auditorium. A producer of the show sat down next to me. "Your old man is really something. It must be great having him for your father."

I didn't know what to say. How could I tell this producer that his star wasn't really a great father? Dad rarely came home from the office before 9:00 P.M., and when he did, he was usually engrossed in some sort of project. My sister and I can't remember our father ever playing with us, or him ever appreciating the value of play. Years later, I learned that his father had never played with him.

My mother rarely played with us either. She had been a career woman, an educator who specialized in teaching the mentally retarded. After her death the school board named a high school after her. At work they called her an "angel;" she was respected and revered for her selfless efforts. Her professional gains were our family's losses. We always had baby sitters at the house to greet us when we arrived home from school, a steady stream of elderly women. These caretakers played a large part in my early childhood. On my sister's fifth birthday, Mrs. Beale, our favorite, took us all to a restaurant to have ice cream sodas at the counter. She let us all play dress up, and I went as a girl; I was amazed when no one could tell I was really a boy. Another day, at nap time, I advanced the hands of the clock two hours by sticking my fingers through the broken clock face, and then jumped up, ready to play. Mrs. Beale, anticipating several hours of child-free bliss, did not appear pleased by my efforts to make time fly. One sitter was fired after she washed my mouth out with soap. Although I no longer remember my transgression, I have never forgotten the taste of that soap.

More than twenty-five years have passed since my mother died of cancer, and my father now is eighty-five years old. He tried to boil a pot of water last month, but fell asleep and nearly burned down his apartment. The apartment manager, frustrated by my father's failing faculties, had his stove turned off to prevent further mishaps. Although he won't admit it, my father is no longer able to live independently. Last fall we decided it was time to move him to a retirement hotel.

As I sat on the airplane, traveling down to Los Angeles where my father still lived, I tried to imagine what he was feeling. I, too, had become a psychologist, and was used to examining people's emotional reactions. I wondered if he was frightened? Did he see this as the first step towards the grave? Would he blame me for not taking him into my house and looking after him myself?

I arrived late on a Thursday evening and stopped at Ralph's Supermarket to stock up on groceries. It seemed impossible to sort through his lifetime's belongings without stocking up on Hebrew National hot dogs and kosher dill pickles. Besides, with my father, nothing you would find in the refrigerator was safe. Even the ketchup, like everything else in the house, was dated.

As soon as I arrived, I sat down next to my father on the sofa in the living room of his cavernous apartment. He didn't look well. He hadn't shaved in days, and a gray stubble sprouted wildly across his wrinkled face. Dried juice was caked in the fold of skin angling away from his mouth, and he had bits of food stuck to his shirt.

"So, is everything ready for the move?" I asked.

"Listen," he began wearily, "I've been too tired to do a thing. Every time I start to sort through my papers I fall fast asleep. I need to have another sleep disorder test."

I nodded agreeably and said nothing. My father cannot accept the fact that he sleeps a lot because he is no longer a young man. I often wonder if it will be as difficult for me to accept my limitations when I grow older.

I looked around my father's apartment and felt exhausted; it was such a mess. Newspapers and magazines were scattered across every surface, like leaves littering a lawn after a windstorm. No one ever taught my father how to look after himself. My mother had always kept the house clean, but when she died all neatness died too, as though her memory could be enshrined in a mausoleum of old papers.

My father's sense of time was forever altered the day my mother died. Afterwards he no longer cared about moving ahead. It was like the clocks in the Attaturk museum in Turkey. When Attaturk died in the early twentieth century, the Turks built a shrine to celebrate his fame and to remember his legacy. All of the clocks in that museum still tell the time that he died.

"Dad, now that I'm here, I'll help you sort through your things."

But he had already fallen asleep. I don't think he really wanted to be of assistance; sifting through the residue of his life would bring up too many painful memories. Who knew what secrets lay buried here?

I spent my weekend going through his papers, a domestic archeological dig. Each pile would begin with a few files, business papers, bank statements and stock transaction slips. Mixed in between layers resembling a finely crafted compost heap, were a random assortment of photographs. One would be of my kids on our vacation last summer and the next would be of my mother and father at the beach when I was a child. This would be followed by innumerable bank passbooks, each one stating that his account was closed. I could only imagine what free gifts he received for the opening of these accounts. Undoubtedly those gifts would be there as well. Even the bathtub was full of papers. I couldn't see any of the enamel of the tub.

In one box, buried under a sheath of telephone bills from 1973, I uncovered an autobiography entitled "From the Beginning." My father wrote it in 1947. It was scrawled in pencil on now-yellowed paper, and was folded over. I started to read it, but realized that it needed to be savored and so set it aside for later.

That night, as I wearily crawled under the afghan on my father's ancient sofa, I pulled out the autobiography. Although it was written the year I was born, no mention was made of my impending arrival. Instead, it told of his birth in Kishinev, Russia, and his journey across the ocean and entry to the United States through Ellis Island in 1913 when he was only five years old. But on the second page, just after describing his first day in public school in Providence, Rhode Island, was the buried bombshell.

"Sometime during this period," he wrote, "I recall a sex experience with an older person which is hard to put on paper." Nothing more was written.

I slept uneasily that night, waking up frequently; the sheet kept getting tangled around my thrashing limbs, straight-jacketing me. The next morning we began packing his possessions onto the truck. By mid-morning we had loaded most of his things and were ready. He and I got into his car, pulled out of his garage, and slowly began to make the pilgrimage.

"Dad," I began, in a voice I almost didn't recognize, "I read your autobiography last night."

"What autobiography?" he asked, a blank look on his tired face.

"The one entitled 'From the Beginning' that you wrote in 1947. You mentioned having a sex experience with an older person but didn't mention any details. What actually happened?" I could feel my heart pounding. My skin felt like it was on fire and I wanted to plug my ears. Although I was used to hearing about childhood abuse in my professional psychological practice, I never imagined that one day I would be listening to my father's own story. I couldn't stand not knowing, but knowing seemed almost as bad.

"It happened with an older man, a friend of the family," he stated, with hardly a trace of emotion in his voice.

"What happened?" I asked again.

"He bungholed me." He stated it without denial, with no shame, just like that. He *bungholed* me. I had never heard that expression before, but knew what he was saying. I had thought we would discuss his feelings about being moved into a retirement hotel. Instead, I was desperate to talk about his being bungholed nearly eighty years ago.

"How did it happen?"

"I didn't know what was happening. I guess I was sitting on his lap, and then he asked me to pull down my pants. It all happened very quickly. Then I wiped myself and pulled up my pants. I never even thought about it again." He could have been talking about taking out the garbage yesterday, or brushing his teeth last night. He was so matter-of-fact.

His downplaying of the incident left me puzzled. I couldn't imagine a psychologist who wouldn't explore the significance of such an event. On the other hand, my father has always believed that people spend far too much time "contemplating their navels." He prides himself on being "thick-skinned," which is his way of surviving failure and defeat. I always thought this was the result of being an immigrant and a survivor of the Great Depression.

"Did you tell anyone?"

"No."

And that was that. He turned away and looked out the window, apparently staring at the traffic. It reminded me of that day years ago when we drove to the television studio. I wondered if he was watching his childhood pass by as he stared out the window.

We were going sixty miles per hour heading for his new home. Instead of moving ahead, we were looking back. It was hard to picture him as a little boy, helpless, violated. He had always been stern and gruff.

We were too busy to talk about this again that day, and by evening I was on my way to the airport, heading back to Seattle. He was settled comfortably in his retirement room. I felt completely unsettled, even though my task had been accomplished.

I walked through the airport and checked my bags at the counter. The Super Bowl was on the large T.V. screen in the bar and people were absorbed in the game. I boarded my plane, which was nearly empty, and took my seat. We took off. Everything seemed just the way it should be. The stewardess rolled the drink cart down the aisle and asked if I wanted something to drink. I looked up at her with mournful eyes. I wanted to tell her all about my discovery, wanted to lean on her, have her sit down next to me, put her arm around my shoulder, let me sob on her uniform. Instead, I shook my head and thanked her for offering.

Absentmindedly, I found myself picking up my father's autobiography and re-reading it. I sat absorbed, unaware of anything else except the words I was reading and my own internal images of helplessness. Then, tears began to pour down my cheeks. A deep sob, then another, and then an entire series bellowed forth as if there were no tomorrow.

I wasn't grieving for my father, who dismissed the event as if it never happened. Or for his lost innocence. My father's story could also have been my story. I was grieving for the child I had once been, the one who had never been taken care of, the one who always came home to an empty house, the one who was rarely hugged. My mouth felt dry and sticky; that soapy taste was there again.

I thought of my youngest son Benjamin. Would this be his story one day? A whole new wave of tears began to well up and flow freely as I pictured him in the story that my father had told. It was unbearable, the depth of sorrow I felt for an event that I hoped would never happen. I felt ashamed of my feelings, and was relieved that the noise of the plane drowned out my cries. No one noticed.

The plane landed and I lugged my bags down the walkway and there in the waiting area were my wife and son Benjamin, smiling expectantly. I ran up and threw my arms around him and began to sob again.

"Are you all right?" my wife asked, concerned and surprised.

I looked up at her and nodded yes, not yet realizing that I wouldn't be all right for some time to come. For days we would sit up late into the night talking about my father's secret, trying to understand and put it to rest.

But that day, at the airport, after I'd left my father in his rest home, all I could do was hold my own son—and tell him he was my beloved. I hugged him close, as though by my embrace I could protect him as no one had protected my father.

Stretching

the

Map

Carol Lanie Riley

Out beyond ideas of wrongdoing and rightdoing,
there is a field. I'll meet you there.
— Rumi

Twirling solemnly in Sufi dances has soothed my heart, listening to a guru high in the Alps has moved my mind, and chanting Sanskrit words into the night with Seattle friends has brought me unity. I turned to adventure and a search for the sacred when my sons, whom I had raised to the ages of fourteen and fifteen, moved in with their dad for the first time. In June, I took leave from the corporate career that had supported the three of us.

Mystical pursuits beckoned to me that summer of 1975, the summer I was thirty-three. My mind soared, inspired by the wisdom of Eastern masters. A string inside me was plucked that had never before vibrated. A month after I left my job, I stood on a tiny wooden platform high in the Alps, at the Camp of the Eagles, the international camp of the Sufis. I had arrived there by a series of spontaneous decisions made in the previous several weeks. The thirty-foot square platform where I stood was perched just a dozen yards from the edge of the narrow, plunging valley that separated this mountain ridge from the huge Mont Blanc glacier. I began moving through the slow motions of walking meditation as thousands of snow crystals on the glacier across from me twinkled in the rising sun. Tension drained from me, and my heart sang as I sensed a wondrous presence around me.

I didn't know then that my budding connection with a loving spiritual presence would soon comfort me as I lost one son, nor would I have guessed that religion would cause me to almost lose the other.

In August, the day after I returned from the Alps, my younger son, Danny, was diagnosed with leukemia. Danny, still fourteen, moved back home and my life became keenly focused on him. Michael returned in late fall. One year later, after a courageous fight, Danny let go of his life, as I sat, wide open, holding his hand. Michael shared this loss with me, but we have seldom mentioned the hurt of that year to each other aloud.

I delved more deeply into Eastern religion, became vegetarian, and searched for understanding in the teachings of masters. A refined euphoria gentled my grieving heart when I meditated, chanted, or joined in Sufi dancing. Michael stayed clear of anything with spiritual overtones. He found his relief with friends.

At dinnertime, Michael would sit down at the circular picnic table in the kitchen, with our new housemate, Bruce, and me. Next to the chopsticks at his placesetting, he would add a fork. We would form a circle by holding hands, then begin intoning "Oummmm," a Hindu name for God. At least, Bruce and I would chant. Michael would wait with resignation until the sound trailed off and we began to eat. He would often drop hands, gently pushing away the plate heaped with veggies and rice, lightly joking, but maintaining his distance. "That's your trip, Mom. I'm going to McDonald's."

These days, my grown son warmly holds his hand out for me at his dinner table to include me in his family's Christian prayer.

"Christianity's too masculine for me, so structured and directive," I have said to my friends. "But to each his own," I add, knowing the born-again Christians do not reciprocate the sentiment. I am troubled by their desire to use legal means to force their values on others. When Michael was twenty-eight, he invited me to Calvary Fellowship. I inwardly shook my head, but decided to go, appreciating his offer to share a part of his life with me.

At Michael's Fundamentalist church I stood beside him singing the simple words about salvation that were projected on a screen at the front of the auditorium. A talented pianist spun circles of crystal notes around the droning melody while the guitar player, the bassist, and the drummer stuck to the straight and narrow. As I tried on words about the

Savior and the Lamb, I looked around at the young congregation. Fascinated, I watched the hands of the deaf-interpreter fluidly translate both the words and the rhythm of the song. I noticed a small contingent of people in wheel chairs and nodded to myself, noting that the church did embrace diversity. But my approval turned to consternation when I read the Sunday bulletin in my hands.

"This is interesting, Michael," I commented, trying to sound casual as we stood after the last prayer. I thunked my forefinger at the offending words on the bulletin. On the back page was a list of the support groups offered by the church: Recovering Drug Addicts, Recovering Alcoholics, Recovering Gays and Lesbians, and Recovering New Agers. Although not a "New Ager" myself, I was insulted by the notion that one needed to "recover" from convictions other than Christianity. Aware of my role as a guest in my son's territory, I tried to restrain my indignation.

"I see it, Mom," Michael acknowledged in a wary voice, turning toward me as we stood there in front of our auditorium seats. His eyes met mine, his neutral expression matched my own. Michael's new friends were filing out, and we leaned back against our folded seats to let them pass. After the row emptied, Michael said, "I'm sorry if that offends you, Mom. Is there anything you want to say about it?"

"I can't believe they would put these last two categories with the first two." I shrugged. He knew I had gay friends. "Recovering Gays and Lesbians? *Recovering?*" I could feel my engine heating up, and having expressed myself sufficiently on this ludicrous idea for a support group, I stopped myself. Michael still stood facing me, arms quiet at his sides.

"Go ahead, Mom," he invited. I noticed his gray sweater with the six large diamonds that spread across his chest, and I felt a surge of love for him. He seemed so transparent to me, and so dear, I thought. I wondered if all mothers felt this about their grown children. My thoughts calmed me.

"Mom?" Michael called my attention back to the auditorium.

I glanced at him, and shook my head slightly. Disputing a line in the bulletin was not the way I wanted to enter into dialogue about this church. "I don't need to say anything more, thanks. Ready?" Michael nodded. We turned in unison to pick up our coats from the seats behind us, and moved out of the auditorium.

A few weeks later Michael came over a little after 10:00 on a Friday night. When I opened the door to his double knock, I saw he was animated, full of laughter, more buoyant than I had seen him in a long time. He had just come from Friday Night Career and College Group at church, and had dropped by on his way home.

"Hi, Mom. I thought I'd take a chance and see if you were home. What are you up to?" We saw each other every few weeks, and this unexpected visit was a treat. He put his arms around me and gave me one of his big bear hugs.

"Actually, I'm just finishing off this chocolate Häagen-Dazs! And, trying to stay awake long enough to finish the chapter I'm reading."

I held up the bowl of ice cream. "Want some?"

Michael looked at me teasingly. "Sure. If you have any

left."

I took the nearly empty carton out of the freezer, and scraped the sides and bottom of the container to fill his bowl.

"Do you remember this?" I asked, tossing my head in the direction of the record player. John Lennon was advising plaintively, "Whatever Gets You Thru the Night."

"Of course I remember," Michael replied, casually. "I gave it to you after Danny died."

"Why did you pick this record?" I was suddenly curious, all these years later, why he had chosen this particular record.

"Because when it came on the radio, you got up and danced for the first time in months. It made you happy." Often over the years, Michael, Danny, and I had danced hard together, singing the rock-and-roll lyrics in unison.

I touched his shoulder, moved by his explanation.

"I'm throwing out all of my tapes," he announced, plunking down in a kitchen chair. "I don't want to hear any of that music. It's a bad influence on me."

"Really?" I paused in my reach for the cookie jar. He loved his music. Music was his friend, his stimulation, even his therapy. A beloved collection of fourteen years is no small thing to toss out.

"The Bible says that to come to Christ you must bring a clean vessel, you must burn the vessel clean. That means discarding all possessions that aren't Christian."

"Why don't you just put them away somewhere; you might want them later. You can put them in the shed out back," I offered. I stuck a cookie into the mound of ice cream at a jaunty angle, and handed him the bowl.

"Thanks," he accepted the ice cream. "No, they're

history. Too many memories. Parties . . . girl friends. . . ."

"Explain this to me," I requested, licking the last dollop of chocolate off the serving spoon. Michael led the way into the living room, where a faint hint of jasmine incense sweetened the air.

"It takes effort to change." Michael seemed pleased to tell me ideas he had been discussing at church. "Things keep doing what they have done before, it's nature, and you have to exert yourself to change. A meteor in space keeps going forever in the same direction unless another force is exerted." I could see he earnestly wanted me to understand.

"Burning the vessel clean is like that first moment after the explosion of an atom bomb, when everything turns white, pure white. An enormous change is required."

I sat down on the sofa, refraining from comment.

"And," he paused, sitting down in his customary place, the rotating chair next to the sofa, "it means letting go of all friendships that pull me toward unchristian behavior. You know, like the partying I've done for years with buddies." He munched his cookie hungrily.

I sat silent on the sofa, thinking about the buddies to whom he referred.

"Michael, this is radical. Are you going to change your entire circle of friends?" I couldn't imagine that he would leave his oldest friends, but he seemed to be making that choice.

"If they want to come to church, I'd love to bring them. Nothing would make my heart happier than for Nate to join me. Actually, Nate is Mormon, so I can keep him in my life. But I don't want to drink beer with Nate. I don't want to smoke dope with Dale. I have to purge everything that is bad for me." He seemed to run out of steam and fell silent, looking pensively at the floor.

So many conversations had been shared between us here. I settled back into the sofa pillows, savoring the comfortable familiarity of hashing things out with my son. The refrigerator hummed into the pause. The next record dropped down on the turntable. Van Morrison sang about sliding down a dark alley with a woman, talking her into his apartment. We both loved this album; it has such gutsy rhythm, such soul. This is the kind of tape he'll throw out, I mused.

Michael pressed his foot into the rug, rotating his chair slowly back and forth. "Mom, I've learned so many things. I now believe in the existence of absolute evil. There is an intrinsic force of evil in the world."

"I do believe there is the absence of good, an absence of *light*," I responded.

"It's different," he declared. I have since learned from Michael that my paraphrases are categorically wrong when I use my own vocabulary.

"I now know," he said, "that I'm visiting here. I'm here to do work, but I don't *belong* on earth."

"The Buddhists believe we are here to learn and progress," I said. "It's the same thing: the idea of having a life beyond this one, before and after it, and progressing, hopefully, in this lifetime. That's where karma comes in." I stood and led the way back to the kitchen, to wash up our dishes.

Running his right hand along his jaw, Michael's eyes focused on some spot in the air five feet in front of him, and he stood silent, weighing his words carefully. "It's not the same," he said quietly, "not the same."

"True, we are looking at it from different levels, but how is it fundamentally different?" I was never a mother who baked pies and pressed pants. My parenting gift had been to teach Michael to think. My mind was alert now, ready for a good debate.

Michael's silence was loud as he pulled the dish towel off the towel ring.

I launched into one of my favorite theories as I squirted dish soap into the bowls. "Any religion is just one culture's way of explaining what our minds can't comprehend. Bottom line, all religions that I'm familiar with have the same purposes: to give a way to speak of the inexpressible; to bring solace and meaning; and to set down clear guidelines for living."

I placed a clean bowl in the dish rack. Michael dried the bowl and added it to the stack of bowls in the cupboard with a quiet clack. I wondered to myself why we were often so sober in our conversations together.

Standing next to me, Michael sighed quietly, and called out in a level voice, "Mom? I'm going to be baptized on November first. I would like you to come, if you will."

His cautious tone was puzzling. I stopped washing for a moment as I scanned the silence between us to learn what was unspoken.

"Yes, Michael, I'd like to come. Thank you for the invitation," I reassured him. "I respect you for committing to your beliefs: I know your church is important to you." I also applauded his decision because I saw him reaching for a way to heal an anguish I had sensed in him for years.

Six weeks later, with a lovely Indian summer over, the

weather had become the gray, prolonged drizzle for which Seattle is famous. November first blew in with gusts of wind that stirred the leaves outside the public swimming pool where the baptism was to take place. My son and four other young men were to be baptized that Sunday afternoon into the Calvary Fellowship. My mother and I walked into the cavernous room and moved toward the other guests along the perimeter of the pool. I felt dwarfed by the huge, humid room. The warmth of the room engulfed us like a steambath, contrasting with the chill of the day outside. People stood in little clusters, talking quietly. Mother and I walked carefully to a spot along the pool's edge to stand, mincing so we didn't slip on the tile. I was wearing high heels and my footing was unsteady as I prepared to watch my son move into his new life. Behind the lifeguard platform, a sign commanded, "No Running!" I felt vulnerable, subject to slipping and falling, as if I were one of those delinquents who, despite the sign, ran, and fell.

An odd sensation, I thought, as I recalled walking firmly over these same tiles with bare feet the previous year, heading into the water for my twice-weekly lap swim. As I would settle into my aerobic pace, arms rhythmically reaching ahead of me in the chlorinated water, my mind would start to flow. Little did I know as I swam here for a healthy body, and to cleanse my feelings, that my son would smell the same chlorine as he came here to cleanse his soul.

Swimming overhand laps, I sometimes thought of the pain I sensed behind my son's ready laugh. I felt we had many unspoken topics between us. I found myself lamenting the silence we conspired to continue. Turning neatly at the end of the lane, I would ask myself, Is this lack of communication really a mother-son thing, or is it a male-female thing? Michael had let me know when he was twelve that he was ready to pull away into adolescent privacy. I had learned to honor his right to privacy, although with my parental need for information, the line was hard to draw.

To catch more water, I would cup my hand tightly as I pulled down and back. I would recall our brief one-sided conversations in his teen years, which were conducted in the kitchen as he hurried through from his room to say he was on his way out. He would stand in the kitchen doorway, glancing over his shoulder at me, waiting for the first possible chance to exit.

Returning from my reverie, I glanced around and saw that a group of young men, Michael among them, stood on the far edge of the pool talking. Michael looked over and our eyes met. He smiled welcome for a minute, to which I raised my hand and waved my fingers.

"Do you see Michael over there, Mother?" I asked, pointing across the pool.

"No." Mother squinted her eyes as she looked. "Oh, is that him with the blue shirt?"

"Yeah. Do you think they're going to change to swim trunks?" Michael always kept his in the car, ready for one of the night swims he liked to organize. My chest had tightened when he had told me he sometimes swam alone at night, out across Haller Lake.

"I have no idea," my mother declared, responding to my question. "This kind of baptism is a new one on me! I don't understand the way his church does things. But Michael likes it. Our boy is making up his own mind."

Mother, at age seventy-three, had learned that life flowed better if she accepted things at face value.

The ceremony was to start in five more minutes. Standing with Mother at some random point midway along the side of the pool, I felt vaguely placed. Chlorine etched my nostrils, and my mind returned to those bi-weekly swims. I would order myself to pull more strongly from the shoulder, keep my legs straight at the knee, as I cruised through the water. I loved seeing the surface of the water go skimming by at eye-level, as if I were swimming at terrific speed.

As I swam, I would reflect on our silence after Danny's death. I found being immersed in water, swimming the side stroke, the most comforting time to allow myself to think of that impossible era twelve years before. If tears came, they could slide into the pool. I would feel my way through the last year of Danny's life, reliving that year as if I could change it, and I would wonder what had been going on for Michael as I battled by Danny's side. Michael, at sixteen, had been left to cook his own meals, wash his own clothes, and run his own life, with little support for his grief. After Danny's death, Michael, a congenial leader among his friends, leaned heavily into friendship, marijuana, and rock-and-roll for his escape. Our communication became perfunctory as he pushed away from the closeness the three of us had shared.

Michael skipped high school often, and seemed to enjoy daredevil acts. Once, he was picked up by the police for siphoning gas out of a car parked in front of the owner's home. Another time, he jumped from the second story window of a deserted Army building after breaking in with a group of friends. His closest buddies, who called themselves "Riley's Renegades," had given him the nickname "Wildman." When I thought about Michael's recklessness I would switch to the Australian crawl, pulling myself along the blue line below me in the pool as fast as I could, scared by the way he ignored danger.

The blue line I was staring at on the pool floor undulated, and my attention returned to the baptism. The group of men was silently beginning to enter the pool, fully clothed. The assistant pastor, who was presiding over the baptism, began to speak and silence spread around the edge of the pool. My son entered the pool in bare feet, the dazzling smile beneath his red moustache lighting up his face.

"Michael Riley," the assistant pastor intoned. My son waded toward the two helpers who stood thigh-deep in the pool, his 185-pound frame pushing a ripple of water ahead of him.

"Michael is turning a page in his life and leaving behind earthly habits that were pulling him down." I surmised that the assistant pastor was referring to Michael's serious marijuana habit and to his loss of chastity. I thought about his tape collection.

"Michael enters his life as a child of God . . . with *faith!*" I silently agreed. My son seemed to be on the edge of his world looking for answers and taking a prayerful step into the void. Pressing my lips together into a straight line, I mused ruefully that he wasn't only making a down payment on the Christian life: Michael was surrendering his whole emotional bankroll, reserving nothing.

With a man on either side, he leaned back, depending

on them for support as they held his muscular upper arms. He fell backward with breathtaking abruptness. The water rolled up around him as his head and body submerged, and his bare feet surfaced. The helpers brought him smoothly back to standing and held his arms for a few seconds while he regained his balance. The water pouring off him made a fountain of sound.

In the following weeks, Michael quoted his pastor often. My spine would stiffen at the simplistic ideas, my voice would rise in disbelief, and my son would retreat into silence. I was bewildered to see he didn't question the close-minded view of the Fundamentalists who attempted to legislate away the rights of other groups, and who said their way was the *only way* to God. As broad-minded as I typically am, I discovered, paradoxically, that I can barely tolerate intolerance.

As months went by, I struggled to stop myself from spouting judgments when he implied that Fundamentalists had the only right answers. His pastor told him that one of the actions he must take to be a good Christian was to "witness" so others could be saved. Michael wanted me to have eternal life. I wanted Michael to think for himself. I felt like I was wrestling with the pastor, who stood invisible behind my son. I would try to summon him back to our old familiar form of educational dialogue, tugging at him, my lesson from the baptism forgotten. We talked less and less as Michael spent most off-work hours in Christian fellowship, learning, singing, teaching, and studying the Bible. I began to understand the wisdom in Michael's earlier caution when he spoke to me about his church. Our relationship was in jeopardy.

We agreed not to discuss our beliefs. Michael was circumspect whenever he touched on his faith. We skirted the dynamic topic, but this left us very little left to talk about because his church was his life.

I understood that Michael was seeking a way out of his private pain. Over the next year I watched as the "personal relationship with Jesus Christ" that his church emphasizes filled a black hole somewhere inside him and brought him out of despair. While he speaks gingerly now to me about my spiritual salvation, I feel grateful that he reached for his own personal salvation. "Whatever Gets You Thru the Night," I sing to him in my head, challenging myself to find a place for his beliefs. Our deep loyalty to one another has held fast.

As a mother, I have had to stretch to include born-again Christianity on my internal map, surrendering my stereotyped prejudice against the religious right. Until Michael's baptism the Born-Agains had been *them,* but each time I say "they" Michael gently lets me know he is a part of that camp. I have learned to stop the immediate discount my mind made. Now my only child has become one of them and I have had to consider anew.

When I attend Michael's church with him several times a year, I stand beside him and watch him raise his palms up toward the sky as he chants the simple lyrics over and over. I recognize in him the same spiritual euphoria that chanting Sanskrit words at a Hindu retreat brought to me. Although the energy in Fundamentalism is far different than the energy of Eastern mysticism, I believe my son's search is the same as mine: a search for the Transcendent.

As Michael stood regaining his balance in the pool after

full immersion, his eyes were closed; water streamed from his hair down over his face. His expression was unguarded, shining with a sacred glow. I witnessed that radiance, and my throat ached. He appeared so vulnerable that I wanted to close my eyes, as if to give him privacy. An understanding washed through me that was so potent it was soon to slide from my conscious mind, to be relearned slowly: My role as the strongest influence in my son's life was, unexpectedly, over. I took a deep breath, and the tingling resonance of truth silenced my thoughts. Breathing out slowly, I began absorbing this loss, this gain, while I stood, rooted, watching my son enter his own domain.

My Father's Last Passover

Norman Glassman

It was a warm night in April when my father led his last Passover Seder. Weak with illness, he leaned against the pillows that were stuffed into a big blue chintz armchair. He wore pajamas; he wasn't strong enough to dress.

We had a special guest that year, Dr. Hotchkiss, the thoracic surgeon who had operated on my father five months earlier. Although Dad said Hotchkiss, who wasn't Jewish, was pleased to be invited, we all joked that once my father decided to invite him, Hotchkiss didn't have a choice.

Thirty years ago when I was twenty, and still treated like a child, I couldn't comprehend just how sick my father was. My entire family kept me from knowing. Not even when my Uncle Bill, whom I'd never known to venture beyond New York City, showed up at our home in Norfolk the week before Passover, did it occur to me that he had come to say good-bye to his brother. "Oh, isn't it nice that Uncle Bill came to visit Dad!" I thought.

Birth, slavery, freedom, and a messianic hope for a better world for all people—these all merge through the ceremony. At Passover, we remember the Jews who fled from Egypt and emerged from bondage an emancipated people.

The Seder is a highly ritualized ceremonial feast where certain foods serve as metaphors for the themes of Passover. For example, matzah, the most ancient bread, flat and unleavened, reminds us of the Jews' speedy escape, with no time for the dough to breathe and expand.

Family preparation begins days before the holiday with the ritual cleaning of the house. My favorite plates, used only for Pesach, were unpacked and washed. They were ruby glass.

This was the only time of year when my father was involved in housecleaning. Every year Dad sterilized our regular cooking utensils by first placing them in a huge caldron filled with boiling water. He put large stones and an iron brick on the stove burners whose flames blasted them until scorched and glowing. He then, ever so carefully, dropped them, red hot, into the caldron until the water boiled over. Scalded in boiling water, the utensils were fit for Passover. I was always fascinated watching my father prepare.

He was a wonderful Passover cook. His specialties were three different puddings made from matzah meal, whose recipes he memorized long ago. Every year he made his own horseradish, mixing grated beets in with the raw horseradish root. The kitchen became a total mess, splotched by beet juice everywhere.

Mother's Passover specialty was sweet and sour borsht with meat and freshly grated beets. She'd start early in the morning and work with the flavors all day. It was always right before the guests arrived that she got the mix of sweet and sour perfectly balanced. I get intoxicated just remembering that smell. The color was extraordinary—a deep ruby red that shone in the matching ruby bowls.

Candles cast their soft glow, and tulips, my mother's favorite spring flower, filled the room. As the ceremony began, my mother lit the festival candles and we joined her in blessing them. I loved watching her ritual of drawing the light from these candles toward her face, her soft silky skin and sweet smile now bathed in this radiance.

As my cousin recited the traditional four questions, beginning with, *Why is this night different from all other nights?*, I watched my father grow stronger, more resolute. I saw him move into that special Pesach mood: a bittersweet celebration of God's emancipation of our people from slavery. He became an Old Testament patriarch, explaining the Jewish rituals. He filled himself spiritually, gaining strength to lead the service. In this holy space, he willed his frail body to once again embrace God's commandment to tell the story of the exodus from Egypt.

At all previous Passovers, Dad had been the joyous director, greeting people, hugging children, kissing women, and shaking hands in that funny way he had of shaking and shaking while telling the person how happy he was they were there. "I am very happy to hear that things are good with you and your family." He was constantly talking and telling jokes. He was busy telling people where to sit, explaining how the story of Pesach must unfold.

My father was tall, almost six feet, big-boned and solid, much broader than I am through the chest and face. His hands were peasant hands, large and thick. He had a magnetic personality and a palpable physical power. Until I was much older, he was the only man I knew who was comfortable touching other men. He hugged, he held hands, he wrapped his arm around a shoulder.

Dad's expression was jaunty and his bright gray eyes crinkled with laughter. He could be loud and boisterous, thoughtful when intellectually stimulated, and he was a wonderful storyteller. Rarely embarrassed, he had the ability to sweep others up into his own enthusiasm.

Until he was fifteen, Dad lived in a shtetl in Russia. It was a difficult farming life. They had a fruit orchard and his mother ran a rooming house out of their home. They never knew when there would be a pogrom, an organized massacre of Jews. After my father punched a policeman, the family decided it was time to come to the United States.

When he was a teenager in Russia, Dad had tutored children for the gymnasium, the upper level school. Being Jewish, he was unable to be a student there. In New York, he finished high school at night while supporting his mother and two younger brothers during the day. He loved poetry and would spontaneously recite verse after verse of "The Rime of the Ancient Mariner."

He had an immigrant dialect. I can remember him lecturing me sternly: "Dis time noobody will let you be lazy. So have dat in mind when you're tinking about your work." He always said he was too busy to learn how to speak properly. He actually spoke pretty well, and I never knew anyone who couldn't understand him. He was eloquent in Yiddish, a language I never learned.

Engrossed in these memories, I hadn't realized how far I'd drifted until nudged out of my reverie by a poke from my mother. It was my turn to read from the *Haggadah*, the Passover prayer book: *For in the time of freedom, there is knowledge of servitude. And in the time of bondage, the hope of redemption.*

We spoke of it all on that Seder thirty years ago, as we had every year. But some of us were impatient to begin eating. My uncle was furtively looking for something to eat to quiet his rumbling stomach. Turning to my mother, he whispered, "How long is Eugene going to make us wait before we eat?"

Mom smiled. "You know Eugene. He's going to make us do the whole thing."

We came to the part of the Seder where we bless the *maror*, the bitter herbs of slavery, represented by the freshly sliced horseradish root. Dad, who had just made a matzah sandwich with a slice of raw horseradish, turned to Dr. Hotchkiss and graciously offered his—without revealing the nature of the filling. I saw how big a slice of the horseradish root he'd put on it. I leaned over and gently took my father's arm, and said in a voice pitched deeply and playfully severe, "Dad, don't you dare do that to Dr. Hotchkiss!"

Dad, looking every bit the Old Testament prophet, gray eyes blazing with indignation, said to me, "He must eat the maror. He must understand our bitterness."

More playfully he said to Dr. Hotchkiss, "Anyway, it's not so bad. Here, I'll make a small one for you." We said the blessing and I watched Hotchkiss out of the corner of my eye as he took his first and only bite. I saw the telltale blinking of his eyes as he fought to hold back tears. Everyone else had also been watching; we all began laughing at the same time, and Hotchkiss gallantly joined in.

But, along with the humor and the sacredness of the ceremony, there was devastation.

After dinner when I was clearing the table, I found my aunt smoking in the kitchen. When my uncle came in, he angrily blurted out, "You're smoking while there's a man in there dying of lung cancer!"

I couldn't believe I'd heard my uncle right. I felt lightheaded and confused. I knew my father was sick; I'd been helping to care for him. But I'd never been told the illness was cancer, much less that he was terminal. They hadn't told me, so that my father's illness wouldn't interfere with my upcoming graduation from college. And I had cooperated. What I suspected in my heart I hadn't allowed my mind to comprehend.

My parents were very private people, and we were a secretive family. There was an unspoken rule that children were to be insulated from painful family events. So nobody talked to me about my father's approaching death.

The end of the Seder came, where we sing some wonderful, silly songs, like "Chad Gadya." With each repeated verse another line is added and the song picks up speed. It is great fun to go so fast, sometimes singing an entire verse in one breath. Someone always has to drop out, choking on the words and their laughter. I always raced to finish first, to beat my father. Not until his last Seder did I succeed. But there was no satisfaction in my victory.

As the Seder was drawing to a close, my father began to falter and was visibly in pain. He looked over at me and simply said, "Noeleh . . . come. Give me my shot." My father hadn't called me Noeleh (the affectionate diminutive of my Hebrew name *Noah*) since I was a little boy. I sterilized the syringe and walked out of the kitchen carrying it over my head, in a kind of exaggerated strut.

Standing over him with the syringe, we held each other in our eyes. I brushed my fingers over his cheek and he smiled. Rolling his pajama sleeve up, I took his arm. I remembered the strength this arm once held; how safe I felt with this arm around me. Taking flaccid muscle and thin skin that barely covered bone, I stretched the skin back, pulling it tight, and stuck the needle effortlessly into his arm. I had to be careful that the needle didn't hit the bone of his upper arm, so thin had he become. I prayed I would get it right the first time; there had been times I hadn't. My heart was breaking, but I didn't cry.

That needle bound me to my father, our umbilicus, bridging our shared humanity and all our unspoken dreams. Each time the needle pricked his skin, it also pierced the bubble of my ignorance. Deep down I knew. I knew, and still I denied my knowing.

I refused to allow myself to feel my fear and pain. This refusal distracted me from what I needed to know. That was why I hadn't understood what my uncle had said in the kitchen and felt confused instead.

I could plainly see that my father hadn't done any of his regular preparation for the holiday: no cleaning, no sterilizing, no cooking. He hadn't even made the horseradish! I had looked at my sick father, yet I hadn't seen he was dying. I felt, but I didn't feel. I hurt, but I didn't hurt. I denied my own questioning nature, "Why is this night different from all other nights?" I will be forever haunted by my father's death and by my denial of his illness.

At the end of the evening the surgeon asked me, "Would you like an extra syringe? I have some in the car. Let me go get you some." This was his way to support me. Perhaps he was also apologizing; he knew he hadn't been able to help my father. It was a kind gesture and I accepted the needles even though I had all I needed.

I've thought about why this holiday moors me in the joy of my father's presence and symbolizes for me the bitterness of his death. I'd always felt that as much as my father loved me, I was a disappointment to him—that he thought I was too squeamish and not tough enough. My not being intimidated by his illness was a major turning point in our relationship. And as he saw my strength, I changed how I saw myself. That I could wipe his butt and give him shots was totally out of character for me. The family mythology about the kind of boy I was didn't fit with this caretaking.

There was a lot of forgiveness during that time between my father and me. Although we never spoke about it, there was a healing and a new respect and closeness between us that went deeper than anything we'd had before. That was long ago, and I didn't have the words then to describe what

I felt. That particular Pesach, the traditional ways we remained separated were not there. As we grew closer, I also moved further along my path to manhood.

Every Passover Seder offers the possibility of establishing a new direction and a new purpose. Yet, as we sat together at that feast of liberation, we were all enslaved. There were those at the table who secretly knew about my father's impending death, but denied it publicly. At this Pesach, we embodied the body language of enslavement: false smiles masking fear, conversation too bright, darting nervous glances and edginess. We refused to witness our collective grief.

That Seder just before I turned twenty-one, when I was not yet willing to completely face the evidence of my father's imminent death, I could not fully taste the sweetness of my own emancipation. In denying my grief and in refusing to break my family's code of secrecy I was not yet free. This was the secret that enslaved me that Pesach.

That night truly was different from all other nights. By the end of the evening I could see my father letting go of his resistance and surrendering to his pain and to his impending death. Not in defeat, but in victory, as a Jewish man blessing me, blessing his family and his people. In a way, he was setting me free to find myself. This was his final act of love. He died four weeks later.

Now, each year at Passover, I leave Egypt once again.

On

Finding

Karen Gegax Campbell

My mother is the bag lady of my hometown. Every Sunday, she walks along the streets of our suburban town on Puget Sound—and she dives into dumpsters before returning to her middle class home.

My mother is not homeless nor destitute, although one might not guess that from her dumpster-diving costume: the old plaid flannel shirt she wears as a jacket over an ancient blouse, the faded dungarees that hang in shreds from her knees to ankles, the navy bandana she ties over her short white hair, and the shopping bags slung over her forearm, brimming with the detritus she collects. At seventy-two, she is wiry and energetic.

It was 1982, and I was twenty-two, when I first learned of Mom's dumpster-diving. On a visit to my parents' house, I sat in the living room in my father's brown armchair. Mom opened the coat closet and brought out a dress. "It's just your size." She held the hanger up to her shoulder, pulling and releasing the long, flowing skirt so that it fluttered gracefully. "And green is your favorite color."

Although obviously not new, it had been a beautiful dress, a seafoam green rayon with a V-neck bordered by a white collar trimmed with lace. Mom was right: it was my size and in a style I might have worn to my job as a bookkeeper. I assumed she'd bought the dress for me at a secondhand store.

My mother pointed out a stain down the front of the dress, and apologized—there had been an open, nearly-empty can of tomato sauce on top of the dress as it lay in the dumpster, and she'd spilled it in the process of digging out the dress. She began explaining how the stain might be soaked out, but I could not hear. Her word *dumpster* had deafened me. I felt mortified, as though my flesh were slipping from my bones and I were melting into my father's chair. I wanted to disappear, rather than put on that dress.

But I rallied, enraged. How could she think I could ever wear anything that came from a dumpster? Why couldn't she leave other people's garbage alone? I tried to pass back to her the shame I felt by telling her, "It just isn't done," the expression she had used when I was a child to persuade me out of unsociable behavior. I stormed through the door as my mother called after me, "Some young lady won't be so proud and will love to wear this dress!"

And so my mother entered bag-lady-hood. It is typical

that she will return from a walk, and ring me up to ask, "Does it *mean* anything when—" and proceed to give an exacting description of something she's seen and how it lay. For instance, she may have seen a certain make, model and color of car parked at a particular place, a car that had a license plate on the rear only, and next to the right front tire was a penny, heads up. The meaning of this may seem inscrutable, but Mom persists. When she got back home from this walk, looking out of her dining room window, she believes she sees sampans cruising in Puget Sound. These two "facts" become linked in her mind. She theorizes that the Japanese are landing on our hometown beach, traveling via that busy road past my parents' house overland to seize the White House. The objects she's found she believes are markers the invaders are using to indicate their route; by removing the markers, she is doing her small part to thwart the invasion.

Her behavior, her paranoia, her xenophobia shocked and shamed me. When I would go to visit her and she would utter one of her bizarre statements or try to foist upon me one of her finds, I would get angry and demand that she see reality, the "real reality," the same way I did.

When I was twenty-four, I married. My husband is more tactful than I. He convinced me that arguing with my mother was not doing either of us any good. When Mom would make one of her strange claims, I snickered, or I tuned her out. My mother had been dumpster-diving for a few years by this time, and her finds had been accumulating in my parents' house. My husband abhors clutter, so when my mother would show him one of her finds, he'd comment appreciatively on it, she'd give it to him, and then he'd take it home and throw it away. I grudgingly began accepting her finds, with a wink to indicate to anyone present that I was only going along with this to humor her, that the object was going into the garbage once I got home.

Often I want to apologize for my mother, to explain that she's merely eccentric, to gloss over the dumpster-diving by saying that she walks for her health, and never one to waste effort, picks up trash along the way. I gratefully agree when friends sympathetically suggest that my mother is performing a community service: by picking up litter, she is beautifying the streets of our town; by recycling the papers, bottles and cans she collects, she is conserving natural resources.

And some items are arguably worth picking up. Mom keeps track of how much money she finds, so that my honest parents can dutifully report it to the IRS as income. (One year she proudly told me the total was $9.67.) Paper grocery sacks full of wrinkly, weathered newspapers lean against more paper grocery sacks full of flattened aluminum cans; these sacks define a narrow pathway through the back rooms in my parents' three-bedroom rambler. She sells the aluminum cans to the recycler, earning about a penny apiece. But most found objects have value only to her.

After observing my mother these many years, I formulate rules for myself concerning what things I may pick up. This is what my mother has given me: a preoccupation with what normal people do. Another person might pick up a penny without a second thought, but for me, whether to pick it up always requires justification, and a test of my own sanity.

My mother questioned her sanity once. In 1970, my mother went to church to ask the minister for counsel. Of the three ministers in the church at that time, my mother saw the oldest, the one who was about to retire. "Strange things are happening to me," my mother said. "I don't feel like myself. I think I might be going crazy."

I've often wondered what course the conversation took. The minister must have asked her to elaborate. Often, my mother speaks indirectly. Did she tell him that she'd stopped the milk delivery to the house? She believed that the milkman was poisoning our milk. Did she tell him she could hardly get any yard work done anymore, because so often there were planes flying overhead? She would shake her fist at those planes, which she believed were spying on her, and run into the house to hide.

And how was it that she didn't feel like herself, he might have asked.

"When I'm standing at the sink washing dishes, I have the feeling someone is sneaking up behind me and pouring scalding hot water down the backs of my legs."

I do not know whether the minister failed to recognize the signs of paranoia; or whether my mother did not disclose to him the ways she believed someone was out to get her. When she described this sensation, he must have ignored the "someone sneaking up behind" her part. Instead, he dismissed her description as the hot flashes of menopause.

"No wonder you don't feel like yourself. You're just going through the change of life. Pray to Jesus for help."

She never sought a second opinion. She was devout before this advice. She began reading her Bible daily, taking the words more literally than ever before. Mom led us in saying grace at all three meals of the day. When she would point out to one of us something that was, to her, not quite right, and we would disagree with her vision, she would have the last word, saying, "There are none so blind as those who will not see."

In 1970 and 1971 Mom confiscated several of my toys. It was her way of motivating me to clean up my room, her reasoning being that if I had left a toy sitting out in my room she then had license to throw it away. Rather than motivated, I felt resentful. It was also Mom's way of censoring my activities. I had a wooden cribbage board that my father had brought home from Germany, where he served in the infantry in World War II. The summer I was eleven, my mother confiscated this cribbage board and burned it, along with my deck of cards. Young ladies, she said, should have something better to do with their time than play cards.

I retaliated. My mother's most precious possession, the Bible she'd earned in her third-grade Sunday School class, "disappeared."

About this time, my father, whose high-school education had laid no foundation for explaining my mother's behavior, chanced upon a newspaper article about paranoid schizophrenics. He recognized my mother's behavior. Unbeknownst to me, he set in motion the machinery to have my mother committed to Northern State Hospital.

After a couple of weeks, I decided Mom wasn't so awful. And, I hadn't slowed down my mother's Bible studies any. It was something she'd remarked on, once my older siblings were grown and gone, that the seven Bibles outnumbered the people in our house.

I did not have the courage to admit I had taken it, so I laid the cracked leather-covered Bible with its red-edged pages in her dresser drawer, under her fluffy pink and white sweaters. She found it that same morning, when she was ironing and putting away clean laundry. She immediately ran to my dad, who was working in the garage at the time. "See? Someone's been in the house and hidden that Bible underneath my sweaters."

I was playing in my bedroom, plinking on the keys of a toy piano I had, when my father came in. "Do you know anything about how your mother's Bible got in her drawer? Did you put it there?" He stood across the room from me, leaning his six-foot frame against the wall, waiting for my answer. He studied me from behind the lenses of the black-framed glasses he wore over his tired printer's eyes.

I lied. "No, I don't know anything about it." *Plink, plink.* I chewed on the inside of my cheek to keep from smiling.

There was a long silence. "All right," he said finally, in the determined voice of a man who has made up his mind about something. "All right."

Within the hour a sheriff and a female deputy came to our house. My father met them at the door. I was standing next to my mother at the ironing board in the kitchen, discussing when the turkey and rice soup she had simmering on the stove would be ready for lunch. We heard a woman's voice call, "Betty?" I was surprised, unused to hearing anyone call my mother by her first name, and turned, expecting to see someone on a familiar, first-name basis with her. Instead, I saw two uniformed strangers, both so heavy that the wooden dining room floor groaned under their weight. They had come to take my mother to a hearing to determine whether she should be involuntarily committed. My mother wanted to change out of her housedress into something more presentable for her court appearance; the female deputy accompanied her to her bedroom. We were an extremely modest family, following what the Bible said about covering one's nakedness; that invasion of my mother's privacy terrified me. I fled to my room and plinked out more songs on my toy piano.

That evening, when my father came home, he made phone call after phone call to my grandparents, aunts and uncles, to explain to them that my mother was hospitalized. Our relatives lived in rural Washington state and in Oregon, and long-distance phone calls were a rare luxury, an event usually timed with the three-minute egg timer. I knew the calls Dad was making were especially important, because he did not use the timer. I listened as he repeated the story of how she'd found her Bible and that convinced him that she was insane. He explained that the standard for committing a person is whether she poses a danger to herself or others, and how he had testified that she posed a danger to me because I was small for my age, and so trusting of her that I would not have fought her, had she tried to harm me. From my listening post at the edge of the living room, I took in this information, surprised. Over the next few weeks, as my mother underwent sleep therapy and electroshock treatments, I felt I had put my mother in much greater danger than she ever would me.

All of this led to a crisis of faith for me. How could that loving and caring God our ministers preached about have let this happen to my mother? How could God take my mother away from me this way, when I so desperately needed to be mothered? The only answer that made sense to me was that there was no God.

Mom spent the remainder of that summer in Northern State Hospital in Sedro Woolley. She didn't act paranoid, anymore, when she returned home from the hospital on medication, but, in my father's words, "all the spirit had gone out of her." Mom has never trusted doctors of any kind, because she says they think they are God, and so has never cooperated with any psychiatrist. The medications for schizophrenia have unpleasant side effects. On medication, Mom would be forgetful. Another side effect, tardive dyskinesia (uncontrollable muscle movements), would have her licking her lips constantly, in a doglike manner. Mom has discontinued her medication as quickly as she could get away with it, and hasn't taken medication, now, in years.

My lie, which I believed had triggered my mother's commitment, weighed on my conscience for seven years. I never told anyone. No matter how many times my parents had said "Honesty is the best policy," I had deliberately been untruthful to save my own hide.

When I was eighteen, I told my eldest sister what had happened in the house that morning in that summer of 1971. My sister dismissed it entirely, was even a bit impatient with me that I would bring this up, so long after the fact. "She was going to be committed. If it hadn't been the Bible, it would have been some other thing."

In practical terms, my sister was right; Mom was a sick woman. In my young adulthood, I followed my sister's example and dismissed the lie. Now I regret that the part I played contributed to my mother's suffering, that summer morning. Perhaps my father even recognized the signs that I was lying, but chose this opportunity to get help for my mother. I have come to marvel at my parents' standard of honesty (who else reports found pocket change as income on their tax return?), and how they could have expected that much honesty from an eleven-year-old child.

I have learned that I cannot reason my mother out of her Sunday morning ritual that has replaced churchgoing; nor can I cure her schizophrenia. My mother does what she wants; mental illness is freeing, that way. Perhaps every town needs its bag ladies who mirror the materialism of our culture, and who find meaning in our discards.

One spring evening two years ago I went to visit her when my youngest daughter was just an infant. Although the day had been warm, the evening was cooling rapidly. My mother brought out from her linen closet a flannel receiving blanket. "Here," she said. "I've laundered it." I shivered slightly, as I couldn't help but imagine my mother fishing that blanket out of the dumpster at the day-care center just up the street. My imagination supplied me with the scene, too, of the day-care center workers shielding their innocent charges from the sight of the bag lady sorting through the dumpster outside, and I mentally apologized to those imagined day-care workers, "It's only Mom!" But I accepted the blanket graciously and wrapped my baby in it, seeing it as the best gesture of grandmotherly care my mother is capable of making. I didn't let the fact that this blanket had been someone else's discard spoil my mother's satisfaction in giving it to us. I gave up that begrudging attitude with which I'd accepted so many items from her before. "You can take that blanket home with you," my mother said, visibly pleased that I accepted it.

After the shame, after the arguing, I find myself slightly curious about how she interprets what she finds. I no longer snicker when she comes up with one of her bizarre utterances, such as, "The toe of the sneaker was pointing north," a veiled reference to that Japanese invasion. Nor do I tune her out. In a sense, I envy her her meanings. There was a time when I was fond of saying that I was living in a Kafka novel, meaning that random events happen: a computer glitch here, something lost in the mail there, and one finds oneself in a situation one would never have predicted. For my mother, nothing random ever happens; not a penny can fall without there being a reason. I don't wish to become a conspiracy theorist, and I don't envy her paranoia, but I do feel drawn to a life where every event would have meaning, and I do admire those who hold a religious attitude. When I experience synchronicitous events, or when a dream offers me a tiny moment of déjà vu, I would like to believe, as some say, "This must mean that I am supposed to be on this path." This is the most profound thing my mother has given me: a deep longing for a religious attitude toward life, yet a deep distrust of religion. I am not an atheist, anymore. However, I feel the quandary: How to season my religion with reason? To have faith—to surrender—seems madness itself.

I visited my mother just a few weeks ago. My father was not at home, so it was just the two of us. My mother's interior life is so rich to her, and I so weary of her exacting descriptions of what she's lately seen and heard, that I don't usually visit with her alone. She busied herself in the kitchen, making coffee for us, and I perched on a stool nearby. Mom broke off from measuring the coffee grounds and said, vexedly, "When I was out for my walk this morning, there was somebody walking alongside me, hitting me on the inside of my left ankle with a stick!"

Against the background of aluminum cans rinsed and waiting to be flattened, she looked haggard. She's grown a moustache in her later life, and beneath these coarse black and white whiskers her mouth pursed in an unhappy expression. The way she stood, slumped through the shoulders, she did indeed look like a beaten woman.

Her voice dropped to a whisper. "I couldn't see *who* it was," her eyes widened, as if she might be able to glimpse her attacker, "but they kept right on hitting me!"

There wasn't anybody there, beating on my mother. Years ago, this is the kind of statement that would have set me to arguing. I checked an old response to demand that she see the "real reality," and felt deeply ashamed. Now I can appreciate that every one of us is locked into his or her own subjectivity. I could taste how bitter to her was a dose of my perceived reality. Now I am thirty-five years old and at last I understand that a hallucinated blow hurts just as much as a real one. "Mom," I stammered, trying to find a way to reassure her, "that must have really hurt."

I am sad for both of us that my mother is lost to a world of imaginary invaders and busy-ness over trash. Many times I've wished some found item could restore her to herself; I've wished she could find the mother who is lost to me. As futile as these wishes seemed at that moment, I had never wished them more keenly. But what I have found is the compassion to say, *Mom, I am so sorry for all your pain.*

Zen

Mother

Debra Bohunicky

My mother told me that when I was small, the first word I spoke was *why*. I have been a seeker all my life, always wondering, always questioning, looking for the true meaning of existence, of life, of God. At the age of nineteen, I determined that I would find the answers in a convent and entered the Religious Sisters of Saint Francis.

By the time I was twenty-one, I was in my second year of preparing to commit my life to God as a religious sister. But I was disturbed by a restlessness I couldn't quiet. The community I had chosen was not contemplative. It was a community of religious women who served among the people as nurses and teachers, with only periodic cycles of retreat to draw away for contemplation and intense prayer. In the cloister, the religious were more monastic, more solitary, spending every day, all day in reflective prayer, silence, and meditation. I was beginning to think that perhaps I had chosen the wrong road to walk in my journey toward the Truth. I decided to go to the Reverend Mother at Green Lakes and seek her counsel. I didn't realize then that this Catholic nun would become my Zen Mother.

It was highly unusual for a novice sister to petition Reverend Mother for a cloister retreat period separate from the other novice sisters. In kind for my summer's residency, I would work the farm fields and tend to Reverend Mother's personal garden. And so it came to be, the summer of 1979, that I became a monastic farmer.

The Hermitage was located on a farm owned by the Sisters called Green Lakes in upstate New York. There was a small two-bedroom cottage where individual retreatants could stay. The kitchen was large enough for a table and chairs. There was no living room. As I entered the cottage, I was immediately in the heart of the chapel, a converted dining room. A small wood stump altar, covered with a handmade white lace cloth, stood before the center wall. On this altar of nature and grace was placed the monstrance, the elaborate gold ornament housing the Sacred Bread which we believed represented the Christ embodied. A tall red glass tabernacle candle burned at its side in vigilant honor. Out of respect and reverence, there was only silence in this sacred domain. I felt right at home.

I had a vigorous schedule. Rising before the sun, my

days were spent with prayers, meals, and farm work. Silence dominated the hours. It was hard and steady work that yielded a toned body and a satisfied soul. The farm experience was quite new for me. I was born and raised in a small city in upstate New York. While my grandmother had a lovely garden, I couldn't stand to get my hands dirty. As the eldest of four children, I spent a great deal of my time running after my brothers and sister and helping with the chores. Gardening wasn't one of them.

Since I had never worked with soil before, I was surprised that I was so willing to get my hands into it. The feel of the cool, moist sod under the sun's penetrating warmth created a deep connection for me with Mother Earth. I had never grasped the essence of that title before then. The moist dark blanket of soil was softer than I expected. I squished it playfully through my fingers and watched as the sod filled my lily white hands and nails. I couldn't resist tasting it. The salty-sweet smooth crumbs were a pleasant and palatable surprise. The pungent scent left by earthworm trails as I turned and tilled the land left me intoxicated with Earth's perfume. It wasn't fabric softener and Lemon Pledge, smells reminiscent of my own birth mother, but it *was* Mother, in a sense, for me. This Mother also fed me, clothed me, and nurtured me in ways I sadly took for granted. I experienced a deep growing gratitude and awe, a oneness with this newfound Mother in my life.

I was simply ecstatic when Reverend Mother invited me to tend her personal garden which fed the Green Lakes community of fifty sisters. She needed the tomato patch weeded. I felt challenged by the short sturdy green things in the section of garden called the tomato patch. I went to work, diligently bending down to sniff out the weedy antagonists of the delicate tomatoes. I guessed that the prickly-leafed, acrid smelling plants had to be weeds. Tomatoes were so smooth, succulent, and sweet. These plants that smelled so horrible couldn't possibly bear the delicious fruit. I recalled how my dad would talk about the creeping crab grass in our yard and I deduced that any plant with creeping tendrils had to be weeds. By noon, I had completed weeding out twenty-five of the fifty rows of tomato plants.

Sister Amelia, the housekeeper, came to call me in for lunch. Sister Amelia was quite petite and always looked pale despite the many hours she spent around a hot stove cooking for Reverend Mother and her guests. I stood up with my straw hat tied around my tanned face. Slips of my blanched brunette hair escaped in sun-blonde curls from my bonnet. My red checkered apron was covered with smudges of drying weeds and mud. I smiled a broad silent smile pointing out to Sister Amelia my proud accomplishment. She let out a gasp and scurried back toward the house like a field mouse who had just seen Angel, the farm's feline mascot.

I began dusting off my apron and lining up my tools to prepare myself to go up for lunch. As I laid the last spade aside, I noticed an ominous shadow crossing mine. I looked up to see Reverend Mother. Rising, I signed for permission to speak. She nodded.

"Mother," I exclaimed. "Look how much I have been able to do. You will have the best tomatoes this year. The whole Motherhouse will be talking."

"Yes," she answered in a soft, gentle voice. Her clear

blue eyes carefully surveyed the garden.

Reverend Mother Vincentia was known for her no-nonsense, but gentle, ways. I guessed that she was an older woman, mid-sixties or so. Mother was short and had the tanned, leathery skin of a country woman. She spoke in whispered tones most of the time. Her practice was to look you right in the eyes when conversing, a gaze that felt as though she could see right through you. Sometimes she would crinkle her dark eyebrows together, the only hint of expression outside of her kind smile we would see.

Mother Vincentia possessed a dry, sharp wit and a subtle, surprising sense of humor. A keenly observant woman, she had an intuitive wisdom that seemed omniscient. I admired her. Mother was the master teacher, my teacher, as I would learn on this retreat. She stretched my perceptions beyond my singular focus of one road; I learned to walk the landscape of many experiences. In fact, the learning had already begun. Only I didn't yet see it.

Reverend Mother wore the traditional habit, the last of only a handful of sisters then who wore them. She always smelled faintly of Ivory soap and starch. Mother was impeccably neat. Her white underveil was blindingly bleached, starched to a slight shine, and perfectly curled. Her black overveil creased with a line edge so sharp you could almost cut yourself on it. Never was there a pleat out of place. One of the junior sisters told me that Reverend Mother Vincentia was the only woman in the order who could get her knots on the cord we wore around our waists into three exact distances, a symbol representing the vows of poverty, chastity and obedience. Of the entire habit we wore, that was the one thing I never could master, getting those knots right. I often wondered if that was why she was elected by our community to become Reverend Mother.

"Dear . . . ," her voice brought me out of my reverie. "Dear, dear Sister. Has anyone ever shown you a weed before?"

"Why, yes, Mother. I've been weeding since I got up here." I was innocently incensed that she hadn't acknowledged my valiant efforts.

"Well," she continued, ignoring this slight impudence, "the tomatoes will be poor this year."

I was flabbergasted. "What do you mean, Mother?"

"You see, little Sister, you have pulled up all the tomato plants and left the weeds. It's a good thing you weren't the farmer in Scripture or there'd have been no wheat to harvest." Mother pointed somberly to the neat piles of plant life I had so happily uprooted.

I uttered a low groan. I could feel the color drain from my face. "Could I replant them? Mother, please tell me I can replant them. Oh, oh, oh, I am so sorry." My contrite heart was heavy with guilt.

"Come in, now," she remarked softly. "It is time for lunch. We cannot undo the deed so at least let us nourish ourselves for the lessons in weeding you'll have from Sister Delbert this afternoon."

She smiled a wry smile. As Mother passed by me, a very repentant and open-mouthed novice, I thought I heard a faint chuckle. I was bewildered.

Since lunch was the only meal in which our silence of the day was broken, I spoke openly to Sister Delbert about what I had done. Sister Delbert was a volunteer to the farm every year. She was a jovial nun, short and round with full, ruddy cheeks. Her thick-fingered hands were calloused from her labors. Sister Delbert was fondly nicknamed by the local farmers as Sister "Del." She could be spotted in the fields by her wonderful tattered straw hat over her veil and her blue gingham apron that fastened by large black buttons to her shoulders. She was always chewing on a thin golden strand of straw. Sister Delbert reminded me of a large feminine version of Mr. Green Jeans from Captain Kangaroo.

Sister Delbert grew up on a farm in upstate New York and was regarded as an expert in gardening. She chuckled heartily and explained that I should not worry about the tomatoes. Mother had a throw-away patch every year for young sisters to learn on. If the plants were harvested instead of the weeds, she'd use them for mulch the next year. "A lesson in gardening humility," she explained. I felt a little better, but not much. In fact, I felt set-up, but could not yet comprehend the *why* that was slowly taking form in my mind.

I had always tried so hard to be the perfect sister, the best little nun in the convent. I often found myself in the middle of some messy situation. Once, in my efforts for perfection, I rose so early for fear of being late to ring the morning bell, I fell asleep on the foyer steps. My penance was to ring the morning bell for weeks afterwards. Another time, I wanted to have the morning meal of soft-boiled eggs and toast timed perfectly for breakfast to be hot and fresh. I spent so much time making sure everything was set to go smoothly, I was late for Morning Prayer. In my rush to get to Chapel on time, I forgot to turn on the stove. When breakfast was served, it was burnt toast and raw eggs for the whole lot of them.

Looking back, it seems that I seldom got the big picture. I had not accumulated the wisdom of experience that gave me the vision to see beyond the moment, or to see how each moment affected the next. In my naïveté, I would look at the situation at hand, one generally created by my foiled attempts at impeccability, shrug my shoulders, and store the experience for some future meditation. I didn't know enough to feel humbled.

That is why, when I walked into the lunchroom after my weed-pulling spree of Mother's tomato plants, I wasn't yet aware that I should be chagrined. The lunch room at Green Lakes was a large white room with hardwood floors and red and white checked curtains with matching tablecloth. It was so different from the sterile, unadorned, Novitiate dining room. Reverend Mother sat at the head of the table facing the main window. As the youngest sister, I was the designated server.

I was famished. Sister Amelia was one of the best cooks around and Mother was even better. Mother prepared some of the meal, the vegetables and the peach pie. Sister Amelia cooked the meatloaf and baked the bread. The smells tantalized our taste buds. As the server, my job was to begin the food passing with the visiting priest, then take the food cart over to Reverend Mother who established the order for the passing of the bowls to the rest of the table.

The food cart was laid out like a piece of art, a feast for farmers. In its center stood the rich brown meatloaf oozing its dark, flavored juices onto the large white platter. Around the meatloaf platter, Sister Amelia arranged a ring of fresh baked rolls, nuggets of amber, each on its own white doily.

The sweet yeast smells melded with the juicy aroma of the meat. At the top right corner sat an iced pitcher of pink lemonade. Rivulets of sweet, sticky sweat ran down the sides of the frosty pitcher from exposure to the warm summer day. Just below this was a silver tray of fresh cut vegetables, pale green celery and bright orange carrot sticks, cucumber coins with dark green skins dashed on the edges, sliced cream colored mushrooms and deep red tomato wedges. It was a food garden to behold. In the bottom left corner of the cart sat the most wonderful sight of all. Piled high in a large milk-white bowl were the most golden brown, crinkle-cut, mouth-watering French fries I could ever imagine. French fries were a rare thing for us. I couldn't wait to sink my teeth into them.

I grew up hearing my own mother say that whatever you put on your plate you had to eat, all of it. There'd be no waste for there were starving children somewhere who would appreciate a sliver of what we had been given. This was a convent rule as well. After everyone was served, it was my turn to take what I would eat, a small slice of meatloaf, several pieces of veggies, and a roll. I reached for the bowl of French fries. Reverend Mother spoke up and encouraged me to enjoy what she called her "vegetable of choice." I smiled and thanked her for making French fries, remarking how long it had been since I had tasted them. I thought I heard a faint chuckle, but I was preoccupied, happily piling two heaping ladles of the golden delicacies on my plate.

Reverend Mother began the blessing. "May all present be granted wisdom and understanding to cherish the blessings and lessons sent to us each day. May the veil of pride over our hearts be lifted to see the Oneness of all things. . . ." The blessing closure was most unusual when Reverend Mother continued praying. "May we find laughter at ourselves to be our joy." Then Mother announced the meal to begin.

Most meal blessings focus on thanking God for the abundance of food to nourish our body and soul. An uneasy feeling deep within my center stirred. I ignored it. I was too hungry to heed the warning.

A hush descended over the room. Anxious for that first taste of the vegetable of choice, I didn't notice the stillness. I picked up the first of my French fries in delightful anticipation of what was to come. I bit into it. Suddenly I gasped, choking on the bittersweet flavors that coated my tongue.

"What are these things?" My taste buds revolted with disappointment.

Mother responded, "Why they're French fried parsnips, dear. Aren't they delicious? Parsnips are my favorite vegetable."

All I could do was to swallow hard, smile, and say, "Yes, Mother."

"And they must be yours, too," she continued. "Look how full your plate is, dear."

In a blush of humiliation for my bumbling pride and lack of temperance, I looked down at the golden mound on my plate, forced a weak smile and let out a loud, long sigh. This would be a very long lunch indeed. There was that chuckle again, only not so faint this time. And this time, I finally understood why.

I learned many lessons during my ten years in the

convent. This is the one I remember best because of the woman of wisdom and good humor who set the stage for the learning. My Zen Mother in a Catholic convent led me to experience a most precious gift: learning not to take myself too seriously. She allowed me to blunder forward, looking only at the bowl of fried parsnips and my hunger, instead of seeing the big picture, or taking only a sample before I filled my plate. I came to accept my imperfections a bit more readily and laugh with others in those moments when I was stretched to grow through lessons in gracious humility.

Reverend Mother Vincentia gave me the opportunity to learn the Zen concept of contemplation of the Oneness of our lives, such as I found with our first Mother, the Earth. She also helped me to see how the moment relates to the whole. Looking up to see the whole garden, I might have noticed that the odd-smelling plants were planted all in neat rows, that the whole garden had a carefully designed plan.

Today, at forty years of age, I am no longer a religious sister. I still work in the soil with my African violets. I still walk the pathway that my Catholic Zen Mother showed to me. I now look all about me with a new and growing awareness. I often laugh at myself and find my way is no longer an aching search for perfection. But, I won't eat parsnips.

Afterword: The Gift of Community

Becoming a community happened gradually, invisibly, without planning or any expressed desire. No one said, "Let's become a community," or, "Let's each write an essay about our fathers or mothers." Community came almost in spite of ourselves. It came, not when we decided to publish a book, although that was an important moment of bonding.

Community began when our hearts opened to awkward and painful experiences in our lives and we tried to write about them. At first we wrote in pieces and fragments, not at all certain of what the real story was. As we exposed our fears and our shame, and others read our incomplete documents, we were not rejected. Patient and compassionate understanding allowed us to look more deeply into our stories and discover their sacredness. The gentle questions of others suggested ways of interpreting our lives that we hadn't considered. It encouraged us to rewrite our story from a new and deeper place. When we were stuck, others waited. Their patience gave us the courage to probe more deeply, and the energy to start anew.

As one after another started to write his or her story, it encouraged others to do the same. Soon we were all sharing a piece of our life on paper. Although there were therapeutic qualities to our storytelling, we were not a therapeutic community. The focus was always on the written story, the patterns of meaning, the selection of the right word, the adequacy of the images, whether there was a part of the story that belonged in another chapter, or whether there was part of the story that we had not yet told, and always, whether we were truthful.

The stories are ours. But they are not just ours. The words, phrases and suggestions of others have helped us tell our own story with greater clarity and elegance. For this we feel deep gratitude. Likewise, each of us can point to the story of another and see how a phrase or a suggestion of ours has been woven into the final text. The process of teaching, and being taught by each other, has been deeply moving.

The community we have found is more than a project, although it is that. It is more than just class spirit, or the caring for one another as we have come to know each other by meeting together, though that is part of it. It is more than the encouragement of a wise and generous teacher, though her mark is upon us. It is more than a calling of each other to excellence, or even a calling to truth-telling, as powerful as those callings are. The community we have experienced is a gift, best responded to by wonder and amazement.

—On behalf of our pod,
Harry Applewhite

Contributors'

Notes

Harry Applewhite is currently writing two books, *Walking Counterclockwise,* essays to help busy urbanites find spirit by connecting with the earth, and a collection of stories on aging with grace. A graduate of Yale Divinity School and a retired minister (United Church of Christ), Harry is the author of *Waging Peace, A Way Out of War* (United Church Press). He is married and the father of five adult children.

Debra Bohunicky spent nearly a decade in the Roman Catholic religious order of women, the Sisters of Saint Francis. Since that time, her spiritual and professional pursuits have brought her to her present residence in Seattle, where she works as a nurse consultant. She is writing a collection of essays and short stories about her convent and nursing experiences. She has recently been named a finalist for her poem "Silence" in the 1995 National Library of Poetry Contest.

A native of the Pacific Northwest, **Karen Gegax Campbell** earned both a bachelor's degree in philosophy and a juris doctor degree from the University of Washington. Her visual poem "Portrait of My Father" appeared in the Winter 1994 issue of *ZYZZYVA*. Her essay "Sisterly Know-how" took first place for nonfiction in the 1995 Dorothy Daniels Writing Competition sponsored by the Simi Valley Branch of the National League of American Pen Women. Karen served as managing editor for *My Mother's Tattoo & Other Family Memoirs*. She is currently at work on her first novel.

The journey of **Laura Bowers Foreman** brought her to the Pacific Northwest many years ago. She has a bachelor's degree in forest management and a master's degree in business administration. She credits the breadth of her vision to her Southern heritage, international education, and career in forestry. She lives with her family in Washington's Cascade mountains and is currently writing a collection of personal essays that explore the intricate weave of nature in our lives.

A practicing psychotherapist for twenty-five years in Seattle, **Norman Glassman** leads workshops internationally on men and their relationships with their partners, parents, and children. He has a master's degree in marriage and family therapy from Pacific Lutheran University and a juris doctor degree from Washington and Lee University. "My Father's Last Passover" is a chapter from Norman's memoir-in-progress about three generations of father-son relationships, based on spirited conversations he had with his identical twin sons the summer they turned twenty-two.

Glenn A. Leichman received his Ph.D. in social psychology from the University of London. He has published articles in *The Seattle Times, The Oregonian, Eastsideweek, M.E.N. Magazine,* and *Journey.* Most recently, an excerpt of his "Looking for Pilar" was included in the anthology *Traveler's Tales: Spain.* His work is shaped by his fifteen years as a practicing psychotherapist, his ten years of living abroad, and his experience fathering three children. He is working on *Soul Journeys,* a book of stories about the two years he spent traveling around the world.

Claudia Lewis earned a master's degree in special education in 1972. Fifteen years later she returned to graduate school to earn a master's degree in comparative religion, which led to the publication of "Legajo 162: The Secret Case of Ysabel Lopez" in the Summer 1992 issue of *Lilith.* A writer who looks for the heroic in "ordinary" women, Claudia is currently at work on a book about Ysabel Lopez, a victim of the Spanish Inquisition.

Carol Lanie Riley earned a bachelor's degree at Antioch University and a master's degree in social work at the University of Washington, after having raised two sons as a single parent. Lanie's career path reflects her instinct for systems, which informed her work as a computer systems designer for ten years, as a holistic health educator in stress management and massage therapy for over fifteen years, and, most recently, as a social worker in family systems therapy working with bereaved families. Her poem "Return" is a finalist in the 1995 North American Poetry Contest of the National Library of Poetry, and she has published poetry in several books by Austen Press.

We hope you have found the reading of these essays as enjoyable, provocative, and moving as we found the writing of them.

If you would like to order a copy of *My Mother's Tattoo & Other Family Memoirs* for yourself or as a gift for your mother or father, son or daughter, please copy this page, complete the form below, and send it to us.

- -

☐ Yes! I'd like to order *My Mother's Tattoo & Other Family Memoirs.* Enclosed is my check for:

_____ number of copies @ $9.25 each copy = $_____

Shipping & handling, $2.00 each copy =   _____

In Washington state, add
sales tax @ $.92 each copy =   _____

Total enclosed = $_____

NAME _____

ADDRESS_____

CITY, STATE, ZIP _____

Send to: Pod Publishing, P.O. Box 1124, Mercer Island, WA 98040-1124